Contents

CEDARWOOD

Servings: 1 | Prep: 5m | Cooks: 0m | Total: 5m

INGREDIENTS

- 1 fluid ounce lemon juice
- 4 fluid ounces cranberry juice
- 2 fluid ounces vodka
- 3 1/2 fluid ounces ginger ale

DIRECTIONS

1. In a tall glass over ice combine lemon juice, vodka, cranberry juice and ginger ale. Stir and serve.

A FANTASTIC MARGARITA

Servings: 2 | Prep: 3m | Cooks: 0m | Total: 3m

INGREDIENTS

- 2 cups limeade prepared from concentrate
- 2 fluid ounces tequila
- 1/2 cup pineapple juice
- 1 fluid ounce orange liqueur
- 1/2 cup orange juice

DIRECTIONS

1. Salt the rims of 2 large margarita glasses. To do so, pour salt onto a small plate, moisten the rims of the glasses on a damp towel and press them into the salt.
2. In a pitcher combine limeade, pineapple juice, orange juice, tequila and orange liqueur. Stir well and pour into the glasses, being careful not to rinse off the salt.

CLASSIC BLOODY MARY

Servings: 1 | Prep: 2m | Cooks: 0m | Total: 2m

INGREDIENTS

- 1 teaspoon sea salt
- 1 dash hot pepper sauce (e.g. Tabasco™)
- 1 cup ice cubes
- salt and pepper to taste
- 1 (1.5 fluid ounce) jigger vodka
- 1 stalk celery

- 3/4 cup spicy tomato-vegetable juice cocktail (e.g., V-8)
- 2 stuffed green olives
- 2 dashes Worcestershire sauce

DIRECTIONS

1. Salt the rim of a tall glass. To do so, pour salt onto a small plate, moisten the rim of the glass on a damp towel and press into the salt. Fill the glass with ice cubes.
2. In a cocktail mixer full of ice, combine the vodka, vegetable juice, Worcestershire sauce, hot pepper sauce, salt and pepper. Shake vigorously and strain into the glass. Garnish with a stalk of celery and olives stuck onto a toothpick.

MEXICALI BEER MARGARITAS

Servings: 6 | Prep: 5m | Cooks: 0m | Total: 5m

INGREDIENTS

- 1 (12 fluid ounce) can limeade concentrate
- 3 (12 fluid ounce) cans Mexican beer
- 1 1/2 cups gold tequila
- 1 whole lime, cut into 6 wedges

DIRECTIONS

1. Pour the limeade, tequila, and beer into a pitcher; stir. Fill tall glasses with ice and pour mixture into the glasses; squeeze a lime wedge into each drink.

MARGARITAS TO DIE FOR

Servings: 4 | Prep: 20m | Cooks: 0m | Total: 1d20m

INGREDIENTS

- 2 limes
- 2 tablespoons brandy-based orange liqueur (such as Grand Marnier)
- 1/4 cup white sugar
- 1 lime, sliced into rounds
- 3 tablespoons water
- coarse salt
- 1 cup premium tequila

DIRECTIONS

1. Grate the zest of 2 limes into a small bowl. Cut the zested limes in half, and squeeze the juice into a measuring cup to get 1/2 cup. Combine lime zest, lime juice, sugar and water. Cover, and refrigerate for approximately 24 hours.
2. Before serving, stir in the tequila and Grand Marnier. Rub rim of 4 glasses with sliced lime, and dip into salt. Take another slice of lime, cut in half, slice under skin of lime to halfway point, and place on glass for garnish.

MAI TAI

Servings: 1 | Prep: 3m | Cooks: 0m | Total: 3m

INGREDIENTS

- 1 fluid ounce dark rum
- 3 fluid ounces pineapple juice
- 1 fluid ounce amaretto liqueur
- 1 dash grenadine syrup
- 3 fluid ounces orange juice

DIRECTIONS

1. Fill a 12 ounce glass with ice cubes. Pour in rum and amaretto. Fill remainder of glass with half orange juice and half pineapple juice. Add a splash of grenadine for color.

FROZEN SUMMER SLUSH

Servings: 16 | Prep: 10m | Cooks: 10m | Total: 20m

INGREDIENTS

- 2 cups white sugar
- 1 (12 fluid ounce) can frozen lemonade concentrate
- 7 cups water
- 1 (12 fluid ounce) can frozen orange juice concentrate
- 4 tea bags
- 2 cups gin
- 2 cups boiling water

DIRECTIONS

1. Put 7 cups water in large saucepan, and heat on high until boiling. Add sugar and stir until dissolved; set aside to cool. Place tea bags in 2 cups boiling water, and let steep until desired strength is acquired.
2. In a large bowl, mix together sugar water, tea, lemonade concentrate and orange juice concentrate. Stir in gin. Place in freezer container and freeze overnight.
3. To serve, Place several scoops into a tall glass, and fill with any clear carbonated beverage.

BLUE HAWAIIAN COCKTAIL

Servings: 1 | Prep: 5m | Cooks: 0m | Total: 5m

NUTRITION FACTS

Calories: 369 | Carbohydrates: 49.2g | Fat: 6.7g | Protein: 0.4g | Cholesterol: 0mg

INGREDIENTS

- 1 fluid ounce light rum
- 1 cup crushed ice
- 1 fluid ounce blue Curacao liqueur
- 1 pineapple slice
- 2 fluid ounces pineapple juice
- 1 maraschino cherry
- 1 fluid ounce cream of coconut

DIRECTIONS

1. Combine rum, blue Curacao, pineapple juice, cream of coconut, and 1 cup crushed ice in blender. Puree on high speed until smooth. Pour into chilled highball glass.
2. Garnish with a slice of pineapple and a maraschino cherry.

WATERMELON VODKA SLUSH

Servings: 4 | Prep: 10m | Cooks: 0m | Total: 4h20m

INGREDIENTS

- 4 cups watermelon flesh, seeds removed
- 1 cup vodka
- 2 fluid ounces simple syrup
- 2 fluid ounces melon liqueur
- 2 tablespoons lemon juice
- 4 twists lemon zest, garnish

DIRECTIONS

1. In a food processor, puree the watermelon flesh. Pour the pureed watermelon into empty ice cube trays and freeze for at least 4 hours. Also, freeze 4 martini glasses.
2. In a blender combine the frozen watermelon cubes, simple syrup, lemon juice, vodka, and melon liqueur; blend until smooth. Pour into 4 frozen martini glasses and garnish each with a lemon twist.

JALAPENO MARGARITAS

Servings: 2 | Prep: 10m | Cooks: 0m | Total: 10m

NUTRITION FACTS

Calories: 298 | Carbohydrates: 32.1g | Fat: 0.3g | Protein: 0.8g | Cholesterol: 0mg

INGREDIENTS

- kosher salt
- 2 limes, juiced
- ice cubes
- 1 tablespoon agave nectar
- 4 fluid ounces tequila
- 1/2 jalapeno pepper, seeded and diced
- 2 fluid ounces triple sec
- 1 limes, cut into wedges

DIRECTIONS

1. Pour 1/4 to 1/2 inch of salt onto a small, shallow plate. Moisten the rim of two margarita glasses with water and dip into the salt. Fill with ice, and set aside.
2. Pour the tequila, triple sec, lime juice, agave nectar, and jalapeno into a cocktail shaker over ice. Cover, and shake vigorously until the outside of the shaker has frosted. Strain into the prepared glasses, and garnish with lime wedges to serve.

LEMON DROP

Servings: 4 | Prep: 5m | Cooks: 0m | Total: 5m

INGREDIENTS

- 4 fluid ounces fresh lemon juice
- crushed ice
- 2 fluid ounces vodka
- 1 lemon, sliced
- 1 teaspoon white sugar
- 4 sprigs fresh mint

DIRECTIONS

1. In a mixing glass, combine lemon juice, vodka and sugar. Stir until dissolved, then pour into glasses filled with ice. Garnish with a lemon slice and sprig of mint.

YUMMY MARGARITAS

Servings: 2 | Prep: 5m | Cooks: 0m | Total: 5m

INGREDIENTS

- 1 (12 fluid ounce) can frozen limeade concentrate
- 4 cups ice
- 6 fluid ounces beer
- 1 lime, sliced
- 6 fluid ounces tequila

DIRECTIONS

1. In a blender combine limeade, beer and tequila. Fill blender to the top with ice. Blend until thick and smooth.
2. Salt the rims of 2 large margarita glasses. To do so, pour salt onto a small plate, moisten the rims of the glasses on a damp towel and press them into the salt.
3. Serve the margaritas in the salted glasses and garnish with slices of lime.

TRUE WISCONSIN BLOODY MARY

Servings: 1 | Prep: 5m | Cooks: 0m | Total: 5m

INGREDIENTS

- 4 ice cubes
- 1/2 teaspoon ground black pepper
- 1 (1.5 fluid ounce) jigger vodka
- 3 dashes Dash Worcestershire sauce
- 3 pimento-stuffed green olives
- 3 dashes hot pepper sauce (e.g. Texas Pete')
- 1 tablespoon brine from olive jar

- 1 cup tomato and clam juice cocktail
- 1/2 teaspoon celery salt
- 1 stalk celery, with leaves

DIRECTIONS

1. Fill a large tumbler with ice cubes. Pour in the vodka, then drop in the olives and the olive brine. Season with celery salt, pepper, Worcestershire sauce and hot pepper sauce. Fill the remainder of the glass with tomato and clam juice cocktail. Stir with the celery stalk and leave it in as a garnish. Sprinkle with a little bit of celery salt before serving.

CLASSIC WHISKEY SOUR

Servings: 3 | Prep: 5m | Cooks: 0m | Total: 5m

INGREDIENTS

- 1 fluid ounce simple syrup
- ice cubes
- 2 fluid ounces fresh lemon juice
- 3 maraschino cherries for garnish
- 5 fluid ounces whiskey

DIRECTIONS

1. Combine the simple syrup, lemon juice and whiskey in a shaker. Fill with ice. Cover and shake for about 30 seconds, until the shaker is frosty. Strain into martini glasses and garnish with a maraschino cherry. This can also be served in tumblers full of ice.

THE MILKY WAY MARTINI

Servings: 1 | Prep: 5m | Cooks: 0m | Total: 5m

INGREDIENTS

- 1 1/2 cups ice cubes
- 2 fluid ounces white creme de cacao
- 1/4 cup cold water
- 2 fluid ounces Irish cream liqueur
- 2 fluid ounces vanilla-flavored vodka
- 1 tablespoon chocolate syrup

DIRECTIONS

1. Chill a martini glass by filling it with 1/2 cup of ice and cold water.

2. Place 1 cup of ice cubes into a cocktail shaker. Pour the vanilla-flavored vodka, white creme de cacao, and Irish cream liqueur over the ice; cover and shake vigorously. Dump the ice and water from the martini glass and drizzle the inside of the glass with chocolate syrup. Strain the cocktail into the glass to serve.

COSMO-STYLE POMEGRANATE MARTINI

Servings: 1 | Prep: 5m | Cooks: 0m | Total: 5m

INGREDIENTS

- 2 fluid ounces citron vodka
- 1 fluid ounce Cointreau or other orange liqueur
- 2 fluid ounces pomegranate juice
- 1/2 fluid ounce lemon juice

DIRECTIONS

1. Pour the vodka, Cointreau, pomegranate juice, and lemon juice into a cocktail shaker over ice. Cover, and shake until the outside of the shaker has frosted. Strain into a chilled martini glass to serve.

AWESOME APPLE MARTINIS

Servings: 1 | Prep: 5m | Cooks: 0m | Total: 5m

INGREDIENTS

- 1 fluid ounce apple schnapps
- 1 fluid ounce vodka
- 1 fluid ounce apple juice

DIRECTIONS

1. In a cocktail shaker full of ice, combine apple schnapps, vodka and apple juice. Mix well. Pour into glasses and garnish with a slice of Granny Smith apple.

CHOCOLATE MARTINI A LA LAREN

Servings: 2 | Prep: 5m | Cooks: 0m | Total: 5m

INGREDIENTS

- 4 fluid ounces chocolate liqueur
- 3 fluid ounces vodka
- 1 (1 ounce) square semisweet chocolate, grated

DIRECTIONS

1. In a cocktail mixer full of ice, combine chocolate liqueur and vodka. Shake vigorously and strain into 2 chilled martini glasses. Garnish with chocolate shavings.

HUMMINGBIRD

Servings: 1 | Prep: 10m | Cooks: 0m | Total: 10m

INGREDIENTS

- 1 fluid ounce rum cream liqueur
- 1/2 fluid ounce strawberry flavored syrup
- 1 fluid ounce coffee flavored liqueur
- 1/2 banana
- 1 fluid ounce milk
- 1 cup crushed ice

DIRECTIONS

1. In a blender, combine rum cream liqueur, coffee liqueur, milk and strawberry syrup. Add the banana and crushed ice. Blend until smooth. Pour into glasses and serve.

LEMON DROP MARTINI

Servings: 1 | Prep: 5m | Cooks: 0m | Total: 5m

INGREDIENTS

- white sugar
- 1/2 ounce lime juice
- 1 long strip of lemon zest
- 1 ounce sweet and sour mix
- 1 (1.5 fluid ounce) jigger citron vodka
- 1 cup crushed ice

DIRECTIONS

1. Moisten the edges of a martini glass with a little lime juice, and then dip moistened edges into sugar. Place lemon zest strip in glass.
2. Combine vodka, lime juice, sweet and sour mix, and ice in a shaker. Shake vigorously, and strain into a martini glass.

BLUEBERRY VODKA MARTINIS

Servings: 10 | Prep: 30m | Cooks: 0m | Total: 7d30m

INGREDIENTS

- 1 liter vodka
- 1 lime, juiced
- 1 pint blueberries, rinsed and dried
- 1 twist lime zest, garnish
- 1 cup raspberry flavored liqueur

DIRECTIONS

1. To make the blueberry vodka: Pour out approximately 1/3 of the bottle of vodka into a holding container; set aside. Score each blueberry with a small nick and place into vodka bottle. With the vodka previously set aside, fill the vodka bottle until just below the neck. Add just enough raspberry liqueur to top off the bottle. Let sit in a dark place for 2 weeks.
2. To make martinis: In a cocktail shaker filled with ice, combine 2 parts blueberry vodka, 1 part raspberry liqueur, and a dash of lime juice. Shake vigorously and strain into glass. Garnish with twist of lime zest.

BAILEY'S SUNDAE COFFEE DRINK

Servings: 6 | Prep: 30m | Cooks: 0m | Total: 30m

INGREDIENTS

- 12 cups brewed coffee
- 1 pint French vanilla ice cream
- 12 fluid ounces Irish cream liqueur

DIRECTIONS

1. Brew 12 cups of coffee. While the coffee is brewing, fill each cup with a scoop of ice cream. Be sure to use large cups (the oversized types you get at coffee houses are best). Top each scoop of ice cream with just enough Irish cream so that the ice cream looks lightly coated.
2. When the coffee is brewed, pour it so that each cup is filled up about halfway. It is then up to each individual to add more Irish cream, half-and-half, or sugar to suit his/her taste.

CAIPIRINHA

Servings: 1 | Prep: 5m | Cooks: 0m | Total: 5m

INGREDIENTS

- 1/2 lime, quartered

- 1 teaspoon white sugar
- 2 1/2 fluid ounces cachaca
- 1 cup ice cubes

DIRECTIONS

1. In a large rocks glass squeeze and drop in 2 eighths of lime. Add sugar, crush and mix with a spoon. Pour in the cachaca and plenty of ice. Stir well.

CUBAN MOJITO

Servings: 2 | Prep: 10m | Cooks: 0m | Total: 10m

INGREDIENTS

- 2 teaspoons white sugar
- 2 cups club soda
- 1 lime, cut into 4 wedges
- 2 cups crushed ice
- 4 sprigs fresh mint
- 2 wedges lime, as garnish
- 1/2 cup white rum

DIRECTIONS

1. Place 1 teaspoon of sugar into each of two 12 ounce glasses. Squeeze the juice from a lime wedge into each glass, drop in the wedge, and add 2 sprigs of mint. Use a spoon or muddler to mash the sugar, lime juice, and mint together in the bottom of the glasses. Fill each glass about half full with crushed ice. Pour 1/4 cup rum into each glass. Fill the glasses with club soda, stir, and garnish with additional lime wedges.

EARL GREY MARTINI

Servings: 2 | Prep: 10m | Cooks: 0m | Total: 2h10m

INGREDIENTS

- 1 teaspoon Earl Grey tea leaves
- 1 wedge lemon
- 2 (1.5 fluid ounce) jiggers gin
- 1 (1.5 fluid ounce) jigger fresh lemon juice
- white sugar, for rimming
- 2 fluid ounces simple syrup

DIRECTIONS

1. Sprinkle the tea leaves over the gin in a small glass, and set aside to steep for 2 hours.
2. Pour 1/4 to 1/2 inch of white sugar onto a small, shallow plate. Moisten the rims of 2 martini glasses with a wedge of lemon, dip the moistened glasses into the sugar; set aside.
3. Strain the infused gin, lemon juice, and simple syrup into a cocktail shaker over ice. Cover, and shake until the outside of the shaker has frosted. Strain into the rimmed glasses to serve.

SIMPLE MOSCOW MULE

Servings: 1 | Prep: 10m | Cooks: 0m | Total: 10m

NUTRITION FACTS

Calories: 192 | Carbohydrates: 17.4g | Fat: 0.1g | Protein: 0.2g | Cholesterol: 0mg

INGREDIENTS

- ice
- 4 fluid ounces ginger beer, or to taste
- 1/2 fresh lime
- 2 lime slices
- 2 fluid ounces vodka

DIRECTIONS

1. Fill a tall glass with ice. Squeeze 1/2 lime over ice. Pour vodka over ice and top with ginger beer. Garnish with lime slices.

SUMMER BREW

Servings: 6 | Prep: 5m | Cooks: 0m | Total: 5m

INGREDIENTS

- 1 (12 fluid ounce) can frozen limeade concentrate, thawed
- 1/2 cup vodka (optional)
- 3 (12 fluid ounce) bottles Mexican beer (such as Corona)
- 6 lime wedges, for garnish

DIRECTIONS

1. Combine the limeade, beer, and vodka in a pitcher; gently stir. Serve over ice and garnish with lime wedges.

SPICY BLOODY MARY MIX

Servings: 12 | Prep: 5m | Cooks: 0m | Total: 35m

NUTRITION FACTS

Calories: 27 | Carbohydrates: 6.1g | Fat: 0.1g | Protein: 1.5g | Cholesterol: 0mg

INGREDIENTS

- 1 (46 fluid ounce) can tomato juice
- 1 tablespoon hot pepper sauce (such as Tabasco)
- 1/2 (10.5 ounce) can condensed beef consomme (such as Campbell's)
- 1 tablespoon celery salt
- 3 tablespoons Worcestershire sauce
- 1 tablespoon ground black pepper
- 1 tablespoon lemon juice

DIRECTIONS

1. Mix the tomato juice, beef consomme, Worcestershire sauce, lemon juice, hot pepper sauce, celery salt, and black pepper together in a pitcher; chill.

CHERRY BOMB

Servings: 4 | Prep: 5m | Cooks: 0m | Total: 5m

INGREDIENTS

- 4 fluid ounces rum
- 1 lime, juiced
- 1 liter lime soda
- 1 lime, sliced
- 4 fluid ounces grenadine syrup
- 4 maraschino cherries

DIRECTIONS

1. In a mixing glass combine rum, lime soda, grenadine and lime juice. Mix well and pour into chilled glasses. Garnish with lime slices and cherries.

ELECTRIC LEMONADE

Servings: 1 | Prep: 2m | Cooks: 0m | Total: 2m

INGREDIENTS

- 1 (1.5 fluid ounce) jigger citron vodka
- 1 (12 fluid ounce) can or bottle lemon-lime flavored carbonated beverage

- 1/2 fluid ounce Blue Curacao
- 1 lemon - cut into wedges, for garnish
- 2 fluid ounces sour mix

DIRECTIONS

1. Fill a Collins glass with ice. Pour in vodka, blue curacao and sour mix. Fill to the top with lemon-lime soda. Garnish with lemon wedge, and serve with straw.

BANANA MARGARITAS

Servings: 4 | Prep: 5m | Cooks: 5m | Total: 10m

INGREDIENTS

- 6 fluid ounces tequila
- 6 cups ice
- 1 (6 ounce) can frozen limeade concentrate
- 2 bananas
- 4 fluid ounces triple sec liqueur
- 1/4 cup coarse granulated sugar

DIRECTIONS

1. Sugar the rims of 4 large margarita glasses. To do so, pour sugar onto a small plate, moisten the rims of the glasses on a damp towel and press them into the sugar.
2. In a blender, combine tequila, limeade, triple sec and ice. Blend until smooth. Add bananas and blend again until smooth. Pour into glasses and serve.

DARK 'N' STORMY COCKTAIL

Servings: 1 | Prep: 5m | Cooks: 0m | Total: 5m

NUTRITION FACTS

Calories: 180 | Carbohydrates: 13.2g | Fat: 0g | Protein: 0g | Cholesterol: 0mg

INGREDIENTS

- 2 fluid ounces dark rum
- 4 fluid ounces ginger beer
- 1/2 cup ice

DIRECTIONS

1. Combine rum and ginger beer in an old-fashioned glass. Add ice and stir.

JALAPENO AND CUCUMBER MARGARITA

Servings: 4 | Prep: 5m | Cooks: 0m | Total: 1h5m

NUTRITION FACTS

Calories: 170 | Carbohydrates: 20.7g | Fat: 0.1g | Protein: 0.5g | Cholesterol: 0mg

INGREDIENTS

- 1/2 cup tequila, or more to taste
- 4 thin slices cucumber, or more to taste
- 1/2 cup fresh lime juice
- 4 wedges lime
- 1/4 cup orange liqueur
- 2 tablespoons kosher salt, or as needed
- 1/4 cup simple syrup
- ice, as needed
- 1 jalapeno pepper, halved and seeded
- 4 slices cucumber

DIRECTIONS

1. Stir tequila, lime juice, orange liqueur, and simple syrup together in a pitcher with a lid; add jalapeno pepper and thin cucumber slices. Refrigerate at least 1 hour.
2. Run a wedge of lime along the rim of each of four pint glasses. Spread kosher salt onto a flat plate; press glass rims into salt to coat. Fill glass with ice and pour margarita over the ice. Garnish with cucumber slice.

WONDERFUL MARGARITAS

Servings: 12 | Prep: 15m | Cooks: 0m | Total: 15m

INGREDIENTS

- 2 (12 fluid ounce) cans frozen limeade concentrate
- 1 liter artificially sweetened citrus soda
- 12 fluid ounces tequila

DIRECTIONS

1. Empty the limeade into a 2 quart pitcher. Using the empty limeade cans, fill each one twice with citrus soda and pour into the pitcher. Fill one limeade can with tequila and pour into the pitcher. Adjust alcohol to personal taste. Mix well and serve.

COLORADO BULLDOG

Servings: 1 | Prep: 1m | Cooks: 0m | Total: 1m

INGREDIENTS

- 1 cup crushed ice
- 1 (12 fluid ounce) can or bottle cola-flavored carbonated beverage
- 1 (1.5 fluid ounce) jigger vodka
- 1 fluid ounce light cream
- 1 (1.5 fluid ounce) jigger coffee flavored liqueur

DIRECTIONS

1. Fill a tall 16 ounce glass 1/3 full of crushed ice. Pour in the vodka and coffee liqueur. Fill to within 1 inch of the rim with cola. Fill to within 1/2 inch with light cream. Stir to blend.

CARMEL APPLE MARTINI

Servings: 1 | Prep: 5m | Cooks: 0m | Total: 5m

INGREDIENTS

- 2 fluid ounces best-quality vodka
- 1 cup crushed ice
- 1 fluid ounce sour apple schnapps
- 1 slice dried apple
- ½ fluid ounce butterscotch schnapps

DIRECTIONS

1. Combine vodka, schnapps, and crushed ice in a shaker. Shake vigorously to chill. Pour into martini glass, garnish with dried apple, and serve.

LONG ISLAND ICED TEA

Servings: 1 | Prep: 5m | Cooks: 0m | Total: 5m

NUTRITION FACTS

Calories: 507 | Carbohydrates: 28.9g | Fat: 0.2g | Protein: 0.3g | Cholesterol: 0mg

INGREDIENTS

- 1 (1.5 fluid ounce) jigger vodka
- 1 teaspoon tequila

- 1 (1.5 fluid ounce) jigger gin
- 2 teaspoons orange juice
- 1 (1.5 fluid ounce) jigger rum
- 2 fluid ounces cola-flavored carbonated beverage
- 1 (1.5 fluid ounce) jigger triple sec liqueur
- 1 wedge lemon

DIRECTIONS

1. In a cocktail mixer full of ice, combine vodka, gin, rum, triple sec and tequila. Add orange juice and cola. Shake vigorously until frothy. Strain into a Collins glass filled with ice, and garnish with wedge of lemon.

RHUBARB MARGARITA

Servings: 4 | Prep: 10m | Cooks: 20m | Total: 2h30m

NUTRITION FACTS

Calories: 210 | Carbohydrates: 30.5g | Fat: 0.2g | Protein: 1.1g | Cholesterol: 0mg

INGREDIENTS

- 4 cups diced rhubarb
- 4 cups ice
- 1/2 cup water
- 2/3 cup tequila
- 1/2 cup white sugar

DIRECTIONS

1. Place the rhubarb into a saucepan, and pour in the water. Cover, and bring to a simmer over medium heat. Reduce heat to medium-low, and continue simmering until the rhubarb breaks down and releases its juices, about 15 minutes. Strain the juice, and press the pulp to squeeze out as much liquid as you can. Discard the pulp, and stir the sugar into the hot juice. Refrigerate the syrup until very cold, at least 2 hours.
2. To prepare the margaritas, place the ice into a blender, then pour in the tequila and rhubarb syrup. Blend until smooth, or until pureed to your desired consistency. Pour into chilled margarita glasses to serve.

STRAWBERRY-GIN COCKTAIL

Servings: 1 | Prep: 10m | Cooks: 0m | Total: 10m

INGREDIENTS

- 1 strawberry
- 2 fluid ounces gin
- 2 fresh basil leaves
- 1 fluid ounce fresh lemon juice
- 2 teaspoons white sugar
- 3 fluid ounces chilled club soda
- ice cubes

DIRECTIONS

1. Place the strawberry basil leaves, and sugar into a cocktail shaker, and mash well with a cocktail muddler. Add half of the ice to the cocktail shaker, and place the rest into a tall glass. Pour in the gin and lemon juice, cover, and shake until the outside of the shaker has frosted. Strain into the chilled glass over the ice, top with the club soda, and stir to serve.

COSMOPOLITAN WITH GRAND MARNIER

Servings: 1 | Prep: 5m | Cooks: 0m | Total: 5m

INGREDIENTS

- 1 fluid ounce Grand Marnier or other orange-flavored brandy liqueur
- 1 fluid ounce cranberry juice
- 1 fluid ounce triple sec
- 1 lime twist
- 1 fluid ounce citron vodka

DIRECTIONS

1. Pour the Grand Marnier(R), triple sec, vodka, and cranberry juice into a cocktail shaker over ice. Cover, and shake until the outside of the shaker has frosted. Strain into a chilled martini glass, and garnish with a lime twist to serve.

MANGORITA

Servings: 1 | Prep: 5m | Cooks: 0m | Total: 5m

INGREDIENTS

- 2 (1.5 fluid ounce) jiggers tequila
- 1 mango - peeled, seeded, and sliced
- 1 (1.5 fluid ounce) jigger triple sec liqueur
- 4 ice cubes
- 1 (1.5 fluid ounce) jigger fresh lime juice

* 1/4 cup mango nectar

DIRECTIONS

1. In a blender, combine the tequila, triple sec, lime juice, mango, and ice. Blend until ice is finely crushed. Sweeten with mango nectar to your liking.

SALTY CHIHUAHUA

Servings: 1 | Prep: 1m | Cooks: 0m | Total: 1m

NUTRITION FACTS

Calories: 176 | Carbohydrates: 19.2g | Fat: 0g | Protein: 0g | Cholesterol: 0mg

INGREDIENTS

* 1 wedge lime
* 1 (1.5 fluid ounce) jigger tequila
* coarse salt
* 5 fluid ounces lemonade
* ice

DIRECTIONS

1. Wet the rim of an old fashioned glass with lime juice, then dip in salt. Fill glass with ice. Pour in tequila and lemonade. Squeeze and drop in the lime wedge. Stir.

HOLIDAY MIMOSA

Servings: 6 | Prep: 10m | Cooks: 0m | Total: 10m

INGREDIENTS

* 1/4 cup orange liqueur (such as Grand Marnier)
* 2 tablespoons white sugar
* 1 cup orange juice
* 1 (750 milliliter) bottle brut champagne, chilled

DIRECTIONS

1. Pour the orange liqueur in a shallow bowl; put the sugar in a saucer. Dip just the rims of 6 glasses in the orange liqueur and then in the sugar to form a thin sugared rim.
2. Divide remaining orange liqueur and orange juice among the 6 prepared glasses. Top with champagne. Serve immediately.

LAUREN'S GRAPEFRUIT MARGARITAS

Servings: 4 | Prep: 10m | Cooks: 0m | Total: 10m

NUTRITION FACTS

Calories: 235 | Carbohydrates: 29.4g | Fat: 0.2g | Protein: 0.6g | Cholesterol: 0mg

INGREDIENTS

- 1 cup fresh grapefruit juice
- 1 tablespoon agave syrup
- 1 cup fresh lime juice
- 1 cup ice cubes
- 1/2 cup triple sec
- 1 tablespoon pomegranate seeds (optional)
- 1/2 cup tequila

DIRECTIONS

1. Stir together the grapefruit juice, lime juice, triple sec, tequila, and agave syrup in a pitcher, and mix with ice cubes. Strain the cocktail into 4 margarita glasses; garnish each cocktail with a few pomegranate seeds.

FALL FESTIVE-TINI

Servings: 1 | Prep: 5m | Cooks: 0m | Total: 5m

INGREDIENTS

- 4 ice cubes
- 1 3/4 fluid ounces apple cider
- 1 1/2 fluid ounces pear vodka
- 1 1/2 fluid ounces ginger ale
- 1 1/2 fluid ounces peach schnapps
- 1 apple slice for garnish

DIRECTIONS

1. Place the ice cubes in a cocktail shaker; pour the vodka, schnapps, cider, and ginger ale over the ice; cover. Shake until outside of shaker has frosted. Make sure to pause and slowly let the carbonated air out of the shaker once or twice during the shaking process and also when you're done before you pour. Strain into a martini glass and garnish with apple slice.

TRUE MANHATTAN

Servings: 1 | Prep: 1m | Cooks: 0m | Total: 1m

INGREDIENTS

- 2 fluid ounces whiskey
- 1 cup ice cubes
- 1/2 fluid ounce sweet vermouth
- 1 maraschino cherry for garnish
- 1 dash bitters (optional)

DIRECTIONS

1. Place ice in a mixing glass. Pour in vermouth, then whiskey, and stir. Strain into a cocktail glass. Add a dash of bitters if desired, and garnish with a cherry.

BUCKET OF MARGARITAS

Servings: 6 | Prep: 5m | Cooks: 0m | Total: 1d5m

INGREDIENTS

- 4 1/2 cups water
- 1/2 cup triple sec (orange-flavored liqueur)
- 1 1/2 cups tequila
- 1 whole lime, cut into 6 wedges
- 1 (12 fluid ounce) can frozen limeade

DIRECTIONS

1. Mix the water, tequila, limeade, and orange liqueur in a freezer-proof container with a lid; stir. Cover and store in freezer until it reaches a slush-like consistency, about 24 hours. Serve in glasses garnished with lime wedges.

POMEGRANITINI

Servings: 1 | Prep: 5m | Cooks: 0m | Total: 5m

INGREDIENTS

- 2 fluid ounces vodka
- 1 cup crushed ice
- 2 fluid ounces orange liqueur
- 1 twist lemon zest
- 2 fluid ounces pomegranate juice

DIRECTIONS

1. Pour vodka, orange liqueur, and pomegranate juice in a shaker, and add crushed ice. Shake vigorously, and strain into glass. Garnish with twist of lemon zest.

PINK PANTHER

Servings: 1 | Prep: 3m | Cooks: 0m | Total: 3m

INGREDIENTS

- 1 cup crushed ice
- 1 teaspoon grenadine syrup
- 1 fluid ounce amaretto liqueur
- 1 slice fresh pineapple
- 1 fluid ounce vodka
- 1 maraschino cherry
- 8 fluid ounces pineapple juice

DIRECTIONS

1. In a blender combine ice, amaretto, vodka, pineapple juice and grenadine. Blend well and pour into a tall chilled glass. garnish with an umbrella, pineapple slice and cherry.

BLUE MOTORCYCLE

Servings: 1 | Prep: 2m | Cooks: 0m | Total: 2m

INGREDIENTS

- 2 cups ice cubes
- 1/2 (1.5 fluid ounce) jigger Blue Curacao
- 1/2 (1.5 fluid ounce) jigger vodka
- 1 dash sour mix
- 1/2 (1.5 fluid ounce) jigger tequila
- 2 fluid ounces lemon-lime flavored carbonated beverage
- 1/2 (1.5 fluid ounce) jigger rum
- 1 slice fresh lemon
- 1/2 (1.5 fluid ounce) jigger gin

DIRECTIONS

1. In a cocktail shaker filled with ice, combine the vodka, tequila, rum, gin, Blue Curacao, sour mix and lemon-lime soda. Shake vigorously to get a frothy head on the drink. Pour the contents of the shaker, including ice, into tall bar glass and garnish with a slice of lemon.

PITCHER PERFECT MARGARITAS

Servings: 8 | Prep: 10m | Cooks: 0m | Total: 10m

INGREDIENTS

- 2 cups tequila
- 3 cups ice
- 1 cup triple sec
- kosher salt
- 3/4 cup fresh lime juice
- 8 lime wedges
- 3/4 cup sweetened lime juice

DIRECTIONS

1. Combine the tequila, triple sec, fresh lime juice, sweetened lime juice, and ice in a large pitcher; stir.
2. Pour the kosher salt onto a plate. Rub the rim of a glass with a lime wedge. Dip the rim of the glass into the salt; fill glass with margarita mixture; repeat for each serving.

OLD-FASHIONED SWEDISH GLOGG

Servings: 60 | Prep: 15m | Cooks: 20m | Total: 1h45m

INGREDIENTS

- 5 (750 milliliter) bottles port wine
- 1 (3 inch) strip of orange peel
- 1 (750 milliliter) bottle 100 proof bourbon whiskey
- 1 (8 inch) square of cheesecloth
- 1 (750 milliliter) bottle white rum
- 3/4 cup white sugar
- 3 whole cardamom pods, cracked
- 1 (15 ounce) package dark raisins
- 1 small cinnamon stick
- 1 (6 ounce) package blanched slivered almonds
- 4 whole cloves

DIRECTIONS

1. Heat the port wine over medium heat until just below the simmer point in a large stockpot with a lid. Add bourbon and rum, and bring back to just below simmering. Save the bottles and their caps for storing leftover glogg.

2. While the wine and liquors are heating, place the cardamom, cinnamon stick, cloves, and orange peel onto the center of the square of cheesecloth. Gather together the edges of the cheesecloth, and tie with kitchen twine to secure.
3. When mixture is very hot but not boiling, carefully light it with a long-handled match. Wearing a heatproof cooking mitt, carefully pour the sugar into the flames, and let the mixture burn for 1 minute. Put the lid on the stockpot to extinguish the flames, and turn off the heat. Let the mixture cool, covered, for about 10 minutes; add the cheesecloth bundle of spices and the raisins and almonds to the warm wine mixture and let it cool to room temperature, about 1 hour.
4. Strain the cooled glogg and reserve the raisins and almonds.
5. To store, pour strained glogg into the bottles, recap, and keep upright in a cool dark place for up to 1 year. Refrigerate the steeped raisins and almonds in a covered bowl or jar for up to 1 year.
6. To serve, pour glogg into a saucepan and warm over low-medium heat until hot but not simmering, about 5 minutes. Ladle 3 ounces of warmed glogg into a small coffee cup or small Swedish-style glogg mug, and garnish each serving with a few reserved raisins and almonds.

BALTIMORE ZOO

Servings: 2 | Prep: 10m | Cooks: 0m | Total: 10m

NUTRITION FACTS

Calories: 291 | Carbohydrates: 48g | Fat: 0.1g | Protein: 0.6g | Cholesterol: 0mg

INGREDIENTS

- ice cubes
- 1/2 fluid ounce triple sec
- 1/2 fluid ounce silver tequila
- 3 fluid ounces orange juice
- 1/2 fluid ounce gin
- 3 fluid ounces grenadine syrup
- 1/2 fluid ounce white rum
- 4 fluid ounces beer (such as Budweiser)
- 1/2 fluid ounce vodka

DIRECTIONS

1. Fill a pitcher with ice, and pour in the tequila, gin, rum, vodka, triple sec, orange juice, and grenadine. Stir to mix, then pour in beer to serve.

CLASSIC CANADIAN CAESAR

Servings: 1 | Prep: 5m | Cooks: 0m | Total: 5m

NUTRITION FACTS

Calories: 204 | Carbohydrates: 30.5g | Fat: 0.7g | Protein: 2.4g | Cholesterol: 0mg

INGREDIENTS

- 1 lime wedge
- 1 dash Worcestershire sauce, or to taste
- 1 tablespoon celery salt, or as needed
- 1 dash hot pepper sauce (such as Tabasco), or to taste
- ice cubes, as needed
- 8 fluid ounces tomato and clam juice cocktail (such as Clamato)
- 1 fluid ounce vodka
- 1 celery stick

DIRECTIONS

1. Wet the rim of a cocktail glass with the lime wedge; set aside for garnish. Place celery salt in a small dish, and press the rim of the glass into the salt to coat. Add ice to the glass.
2. Pour vodka, Worcestershire sauce, and hot pepper sauce over the ice; top with tomato-clam juice. Garnish with lime wedge and celery stick. Serve with a straw.

MARGARITA ON THE ROCKS

Servings: 2 | Prep: 5m | Cooks: 0m | Total: 5m

NUTRITION FACTS

Calories: 317 | Carbohydrates: 29.5g | Fat: 0.1g | Protein: 0g | Cholesterol: 0mg

INGREDIENTS

- kosher salt for rimming glasses (optional)
- 1/4 cup sweetened lime juice (such as Rose's)
- ice cubes
- 1/4 cup triple sec
- 1/2 cup silver tequila
- 1/4 cup lemon-lime soda, or to taste

DIRECTIONS

1. Rim 2 margarita glasses with salt if desired, and fill with ice. Pour the tequila, sweetened lime juice, triple sec, and lemon-lime soda into a shaker filled with ice, hold your hand firmly over over the top of the shaker so the top doesn't pop off from the carbonated soda, and shake vigorously. Pour into prepared margarita glasses, and serve.

KIWI MARGARITA

Servings: 4 | Prep: 5m | Cooks: 0m | Total: 5m

INGREDIENTS

- 1/2 cup superfine sugar
- 2 large kiwis, peeled
- 1/3 cup gold tequila
- 1 cup fresh lime juice
- 1/3 cup triple sec
- 2 cups small ice cubes

DIRECTIONS

1. Combine the sugar, tequila, triple sec, kiwis, and lime juice in a blender; fill with ice cubes; blend until smooth.

TEQUILA SUNRISE

Servings: 1 | Prep: 5m | Cooks: 0m | Total: 5m

INGREDIENTS

- 1 (1.5 fluid ounce) jigger tequila
- 1/2 (1.5 fluid ounce) jigger grenadine syrup
- 3/4 cup freshly squeezed orange juice
- 1 slice orange, for garnish
- ice cubes
- 1 maraschino cherry for garnish

DIRECTIONS

1. Stir or shake together tequila and orange juice. Fill a chilled 12 ounce glass with ice cubes; pour in orange juice mixture. Slowly pour in the grenadine, and allow it to settle to the bottom of the glass (be patient). Garnish with a slice of orange, and a maraschino cherry.

CANDY RED APPLE MARTINI

Servings: 2 | Prep: 5m | Cooks: 0m | Total: 5m

INGREDIENTS

- 1/2 fluid ounce butterscotch schnapps
- 2 fluid ounces sour apple schnapps (such as DeKuyper Sour Apple Pucker)
- 2 fluid ounces vodka
- 2 fluid ounces cranberry juice

DIRECTIONS

1. Pour the butterscotch schnapps, vodka, apple schnapps, and cranberry juice into a cocktail shaker over ice. Cover, and shake until the outside of the shaker has frosted. Strain into a chilled martini glass to serve.

BOSTON CREME PIE MARTINI

Servings: 1 | Prep: 5m | Cooks: 0m | Total: 5m

INGREDIENTS

- 1 (1.5 fluid ounce) jigger vanilla vodka
- 1 cup crushed ice
- 1 (1.5 fluid ounce) jigger chocolate liqueur
- 1 (4 ounce) jar maraschino cherry
- 1 (1.5 fluid ounce) jigger Irish cream liqueur

DIRECTIONS

1. Combine vodka, chocolate liqueur, Irish cream liqueur, and crushed ice in a cocktail shaker. Shake vigorously to chill. Pour into a martini glass, garnish with a maraschino cherry, and serve.

BELLINI MEANIE MARTINI

Servings: 1 | Prep: 5m | Cooks: 0m | Total: 5m

INGREDIENTS

- 1/4 cup good quality vodka
- 2 fluid ounces champagne
- 2 fluid ounces peach schnapps
- 3 fresh raspberries for garnish
- 1 cup ice cubes

DIRECTIONS

1. Pour the vodka and peach schnapps into a shaker with the ice. Shake until frothy. Strain into a martini glass, and top off with champagne. Garnish with fresh raspberries.

POISONED APPLE

Servings: 1 | Prep: 5m | Cooks: 0m | Total: 5m

INGREDIENTS

- 1 cup ice cubes

- 1 cup lemon-lime flavored carbonated beverage
- 1 fluid ounce vanilla flavored vodka
- 1 dash grenadine syrup
- 1 fluid ounce sour apple schnapps

DIRECTIONS

1. Fill a large glass with ice, and pour in vanilla vodka and schnapps. Pour in the lemon-lime soda, and top with a splash of grenadine.

VODKA SLUSH
Servings: 20 | Prep: 15m | Cooks: 0m | Total: 15m

INGREDIENTS

- 2 cups white sugar
- 1 (12 fluid ounce) can frozen lemonade concentrate
- 7 cups water
- 2 cups cold water
- 2 tablespoons instant tea powder
- 2 cups vodka
- 1 (12 fluid ounce) can frozen orange juice concentrate
- 1 liter lemon-lime flavored carbonated beverage

DIRECTIONS

1. In a 6 quart pot combine sugar and 7 cups water. Bring to boil and stir until sugar dissolves. Remove from heat. Stir in tea powder while hot. Add orange juice concentrate, lemonade concentrate and 2 cups cold water. Chill in refrigerator.
2. When cold mix in vodka. Pour into a plastic container leaving room on top for expansion. Freeze or 24 hours.
3. To serve, scoop about 1 cup into a tall glass and quickly stir in 1/3 cup lemon-lime soda.

WATERMELON MARTINI
Servings: 2 | Prep: 10m | Cooks: 0m | Total: 10m

NUTRITION FACTS

Calories: 262 | Carbohydrates: 35.8g | Fat: g | Protein: 0.9g | Cholesterol: 0mg

INGREDIENTS

- salt as needed
- 1/4 cup watermelon schnapps
- white sugar as needed
- 2 tablespoons simple syrup
- 1 cup watermelon juice
- 1 lime, juiced
- 1/4 cup vodka

DIRECTIONS

1. Combine some salt and sugar in a small bowl, and pour onto a small, shallow plate. Moisten the rims of 2 glasses with a piece of watermelon, and dip the moistened glass rims into the salt and sugar mixture; set aside.
2. Pour the watermelon juice, vodka, watermelon schnapps, simple syrup, and lime juice into a cocktail shaker over ice. Cover, and shake until the outside of the shaker has frosted. Strain into the prepared glasses.

ITALIAN WEDDING CAKE MARTINI

Servings: 1 | Prep: 5m | Cooks: 0m | Total: 5m

INGREDIENTS

- 2 fluid ounces vanilla vodka
- 1/2 fluid ounce amaretto (almond flavored liqueur)
- 1 fluid ounce cranberry juice
- 1/2 fluid ounce white creme de cacao
- 1 fluid ounce pineapple juice

DIRECTIONS

1. Pour the vodka, cranberry juice, pineapple juice, amaretto, and creme de cacao into a cocktail shaker over ice. Cover, and shake until the outside of the shaker has frosted. Strain into a chilled martini glass to serve.

CAPTAIN'S VACATION

Servings: 1 | Prep: 2m | Cooks: 0m | Total: 2m

INGREDIENTS

- ice cubes
- 1 (1.5 fluid ounce) jigger spiced rum

- 6 fluid ounces pineapple juice
- 1 cup lemon-lime flavored carbonated beverage

DIRECTIONS

1. Fill a glass with ice. Pour in the pineapple juice and spiced rum. Top off with enough lemon-lime soda to fill the glass.

SHAGGY'S MANHATTAN

Servings: 2 | Prep: 1m | Cooks: 0m | Total: 1m

INGREDIENTS

- 1 fluid ounce sweet vermouth
- 3 fluid ounces bourbon whiskey
- 2 dashes bitters
- 2 maraschino cherries

DIRECTIONS

1. Fill a cocktail shaker with ice. Pour in the sweet vermouth and whiskey and splash on 2 dashes of bitters. Shake while counting to 30. Pour into 2 cocktail glasses, garnish each with a cherry and serve immediately

IRISH CAR BOMB

Servings: 1 | Prep: 2m | Cooks: 0m | Total: 2m

INGREDIENTS

- 3/4 fluid ounce Irish whiskey
- 3/4 fluid ounce Irish cream liqueur
- 6 fluid ounces Irish stout beer

DIRECTIONS

1. Fill a shot glass with half Irish whiskey and half Irish cream. Pour Irish stout beer into a pint glass. Drop in the shot glass and drink entire contents at once.

COSMOPOLITAN COCKTAIL

Servings: 1 | Prep: 5m | Cooks: 0m | Total: 5m

NUTRITION FACTS

Calories: 131 | Carbohydrates: 5.6g | Fat: 0g | Protein: 0.1g | Cholesterol: 0mg

INGREDIENTS

- 1 1/2 fluid ounces vodka
- 1/4 fluid ounce cranberry juice
- 1/4 fluid ounce lime juice
- 1 cup ice
- 1/4 fluid ounce triple sec
- 1 lime wedge for garnish

DIRECTIONS

1. Combine vodka, lime juice, triple sec, and cranberry juice in a cocktail shaker. Add ice, cover and shake until chilled. Strain into a chilled cocktail glass.
2. Garnish with a lime wedge.

SHAGGY'S PERFECT MARTINI

Servings: 2 | Prep: 1m | Cooks: 0m | Total: 1m

INGREDIENTS

- 1/2 fluid ounce dry vermouth
- 4 fluid ounces gin
- 2 pimento-stuffed green olives

DIRECTIONS

1. Fill a cocktail shaker with ice. Pour in the vermouth, followed closely by the gin. Shake while counting to 30. Divide into 2 cocktail glasses. Garnish with 1 olive each.

PIERCED FUZZY NAVEL

Servings: 1 | Prep: 5m | Cooks: 0m | Total: 5m

INGREDIENTS

- 1 fluid ounce peach schnapps
- 1 dash grenadine (optional)
- 1 fluid ounce vodka
- ice cubes
- 3 fluid ounces orange juice

DIRECTIONS

1. Pour the peach schnapps, vodka, orange juice into a shaker with ice. Shake, then strain into a glass. Top with a splash of grenadine if you like.

THE VODKA COLLINS

Servings: 2 | Prep: 10m | Cooks: 0m | Total: 10m

INGREDIENTS

- ice cubes
- 1 teaspoon sugar
- 2 cups prepared lemonade
- 1 lemon
- 1 cup club soda
- 2 (1.5 fluid ounce) jiggers vodka

DIRECTIONS

1. Fill a shaker half way full with ice. Pour in the lemonade, club soda and sugar. Cut the lemon in half and squeeze the juice into the shaker. Pour in the vodka, cover and shake well. Strain into two glasses that are filled half way with ice. You can add oranges and cherries for garnish and make your drink look real pretty but hey, do you really want to do all that after work? Enjoy.

EGGNOG RUSSIAN

Servings: 1 | Prep: 5m | Cooks: 0m | Total: 5m

INGREDIENTS

- 1/2 (1.5 fluid ounce) jigger spiced rum
- 3/4 cup eggnog
- 1 (1.5 fluid ounce) jigger coffee flavored liqueur
- 1 pinch ground nutmeg

DIRECTIONS

1. Pour the spiced rum and coffee liqueur into a glass. Top with eggnog. Stir and sprinkle some nutmeg on the top.

THE ULTIMATE COSMOPOLITAN

Servings: 2 | Prep: 5m | Cooks: 0m | Total: 5m

INGREDIENTS

* 4 fluid ounces vodka
* 6 fluid ounces cranberry juice
* 1 fluid ounce triple sec (orange-flavored liqueur)
* 1 ounce fresh lemon juice
* 1 fluid ounce peach schnapps
* 1 tablespoon fresh lime juice

DIRECTIONS

1. Pour the vodka, triple sec, schnapps, cranberry juice, lemon juice, and lime juice into a cocktail shaker over ice. Cover, and roll the shaker around gently for 30 seconds. Don't shake the cocktail, or the cosmo will froth. Strain into chilled martini glasses to serve.

GRAPEFRUIT MARGARITAS

Servings: 4 | Prep: 5m | Cooks: 0m | Total: 5m

INGREDIENTS

* 1 (12 fluid ounce) can frozen limeade
* 1 1/2 cups ice
* 1 1/2 cups tequila
* 4 lime wedges, for garnish
* 1 1/2 cups ruby red grapefruit juice

DIRECTIONS

1. Combine the limeade, tequila, grapefruit juice, and ice in a blender; blend until smooth. Serve in glasses garnished with lime wedges.

ICE FOR COCKTAILS

Servings: 6 | Prep: 1m | Cooks: 4m | Total: 6h5m

NUTRITION FACTS

Calories: 0 | Carbohydrates: 0g | Fat: 0g | Protein: 0g | Cholesterol: 0mg

INGREDIENTS

* 1 quart filtered water

DIRECTIONS

1. Pour filtered water into a tea kettle or large pan and bring water to a boil. Remove the kettle or pan from heat and allow the water to cool. Pour into silicone ice trays and freeze. Use ice within a day or two, preferably.

THE PERFECT MARGARITA

Servings: 1 | Prep: 10m | Cooks: 0m | Total: 10m

INGREDIENTS

- 1 lime wedge
- 2 fluid ounces white tequila
- 1 pinch coarse sea salt to taste
- 1 1/2 fluid ounces triple sec
- 1 large ice cube
- 1 fluid ounce freshly squeezed lime juice
- ice
- 1 slice lime

DIRECTIONS

1. Moisten the rim of a glass with a lime wedge. Sprinkle salt onto a plate. Lightly dip the moistened rim into the salt. Place a large ice cube in the glass and freeze the prepared glass until ready to serve.
2. Fill a cocktail shaker with fresh ice. Add tequila, triple sec, and lime juice. Cover and shake vigorously until outside of the shaker has frosted. Strain into the prepared glass and garnish with a slice of lime.

VODKA MARTINI COCKTAIL

Servings: 1 | Prep: 2m | Cooks: 2m | Total: 4m

NUTRITION FACTS

Calories: 255 | Carbohydrates: 4.8g | Fat: 1.6g | Protein: 0.2g | Cholesterol: 0mg

INGREDIENTS

- 3 fluid ounces vodka
- 1 fluid ounce dry vermouth
- 1 cup ice cubes
- 3 olives

DIRECTIONS

1. Combine vodka and dry vermouth in a cocktail mixing glass. Fill with ice and stir until chilled. Strain into a chilled martini glass.

2. Garnish with three olives on a toothpick.

SWEET SEDUCTION

Servings: 2 | Prep: 5m | Cooks: 0m | Total: 5m

INGREDIENTS

- 1 fluid ounce Malibu rum
- ice cubes
- 1 fluid ounce banana liqueur
- 1 tablespoon grenadine
- 1/2 cup pineapple juice

DIRECTIONS

1. Measure the rum, banana liqueur and pineapple juice into a cocktail shaker. Add a generous scoop of ice. Cover and shake until the outside is frosty, about 30 seconds. Strain into a glass filled with ice and gently pour the grenadine on top. It should float.

COCONUT MARGARITAS

Servings: 4 | Prep: 10m | Cooks: 0m | Total: 10m

INGREDIENTS

- 2 cups ice
- 1 1/2 fluid ounces triple sec
- 3/4 cup sweetened coconut cream
- 1/4 cup sweetened flaked coconut
- 4 1/2 fluid ounces tequila

DIRECTIONS

1. Fill a blender with ice; add the coconut cream, tequila, and triple sec; blend at high speed until smooth. Scatter the coconut onto a plate. Wet the rims of four glasses. Dip the glass rims in the coconut. Serve the margaritas in the prepared glasses.

PISCO SOUR

Servings: 2 | Prep: 5m | Cooks: 0m | Total: 5m

INGREDIENTS

- 4 cups ice cubes

- 1/3 cup white sugar
- 1 cup pisco
- 1 egg white
- 1/3 cup lemon juice
- aromatic bitters

DIRECTIONS

1. Place ice cubes, pisco, lemon juice, sugar, egg white, and bitters in the bowl of a blender. Blend on high speed until finely pureed. Pour into two glasses and garnish with an additional dash of bitters.

AMAJO'S CREAMSICLE MARTINI
Servings: 1 | Prep: 5m | Cooks: 0m | Total: 5m

INGREDIENTS

- 1 fluid ounce vodka
- 1 fluid ounce fat free half-and-half
- 1 fluid ounce triple sec
- 1 slice orange
- 1 fluid ounce orange juice

DIRECTIONS

1. Fill a cocktail shaker with ice cubes. Pour in the vodka, triple sec, orange juice, and half-and-half. Shake until frosty, about 15 seconds; strain into a martini glass, and garnish with an orange slice.

GENE'S LONG ISLAND ICED TEA
Servings: 1 | Prep: 1m | Cooks: 0m | Total: 1m

INGREDIENTS

- 1 fluid ounce vodka
- 1 fluid ounce rum
- 1 fluid ounce gin
- 1 (12 fluid ounce) can or bottle cola-flavored carbonated beverage
- 1 fluid ounce triple sec liqueur

DIRECTIONS

1. Pour vodka, gin, triple sec and rum together into a large pitcher and adjust the cola proportions to your personal taste and stir. Pour into a tall glass with ice.

RUM ROLLOVER

Servings: 1 | Prep: 3m | Cooks: 0m | Total: 3m

INGREDIENTS

- 1 (1.5 fluid ounce) jigger coconut flavored rum
- 1 dash grenadine syrup
- 1 (1.5 fluid ounce) jigger orange juice
- 1/2 cup crushed ice
- 3 fluid ounces pineapple juice

DIRECTIONS

1. In a mixing glass, combine coconut rum, orange juice and pineapple juice. Mix well and pour into an ice filled glass. Top with a splash of grenadine.

GRAND MARGARITA

Servings: 6 | Prep: 10m | Cooks: 0m | Total: 10m

INGREDIENTS

- 3 cups water
- 1 1/2 cups silver tequila
- 1 1/2 cups fresh lime juice
- 1 lime, cut into 8 wedges
- 1 1/2 cups cointreau
- coarse salt

DIRECTIONS

1. Combine the water, lime juice, tequila, and cointreau in a half-gallon pitcher. Stir to mix.
2. To serve, rub the rim of a margarita glass with lime, and dip in salt. Fill the glass with ice, and top with the tequila mixture. Garnish with a slice of lime.

PINA COLADA

Servings: 1 | Prep: 2m | Cooks: 0m | Total: 2m

INGREDIENTS

- 1/2 cup crushed ice
- 1 fluid ounce heavy cream
- 6 fluid ounces pineapple juice
- 1 pineapple wedge

- 2 fluid ounces rum
- 1 maraschino cherry
- 1 fluid ounce sweetened coconut cream

DIRECTIONS

1. In a blender, combine ice, pineapple juice, rum, coconut cream and heavy cream. Blend until smooth. Pour into glass and garnish with pineapple wedge and cherry.

LIQUID HOT APPLE PIE

Servings: 28 | Prep: 15m | Cooks: 1h | Total: 1h15m

INGREDIENTS

- 1 gallon apple juice
- 1 pint whiskey
- 1 (2 liter) bottle cold ginger ale
- 1 pint spiced rum
- 1 cup brown sugar
- 3 (3 inch) cinnamon sticks

DIRECTIONS

1. In a large pot, combine the apple juice, ginger ale and brown sugar. Bring to a simmer and cook for 20 minutes. Cool to room temperature. Stir in the whiskey and spiced rum and let stand for 1 hour. Pour into 1 gallon jugs or containers and place a cinnamon stick in each one. Cover and store until serving. This can be served warm, but don't heat too much or the alcohol will burn off.

THE BEST RASPBERRY MARGARITA

Servings: 1 | Prep: 5m | Cooks: 0m | Total: 5m

INGREDIENTS

- 5 fluid ounces sweet-and-sour cocktail mix
- 2 cups ice cubes
- 2 fluid ounces premium tequila
- margarita salt
- 1 fluid ounce cointreau
- 1 lime, cut into 4 wedges
- 1 fluid ounce Chambord (raspberry liqueur)

DIRECTIONS

1. Pour the sweet and sour mix, tequila, cointreau, and raspberry liqueur into a shaker filled with ice. Shake until the shaker is frosty on the outside. Rub the rim of a margarita glass with a lime wedge, then dip in salt. Add a few ice cubes to the glass, then strain the liquid from the shaker carefully into the glass. Garnish with a lime wedge.

BASIC MARGARITA

Servings: 4 | Prep: 3m | Cooks: 2m | Total: 5m

INGREDIENTS

- 5 fluid ounces tequila
- 4 cups ice cubes
- 3 fluid ounces triple sec
- coarse salt
- 2 (6 ounce) cans frozen limeade concentrate

DIRECTIONS

1. Salt the rims of 2 large margarita glasses. To do so, pour salt onto a small plate, moisten the rims of the glasses on a damp towel and press them into the salt.
2. In a blender combine tequila, triple sec and limeade concentrate. Fill blender with ice cubes. Blend until smooth. Pour into glasses, garnish with slice of lime and serve.

BUTTERY NIPPLE

Servings: 4 | Prep: 2m | Cooks: 0m | Total: 2m

INGREDIENTS

- 1 (1.5 fluid ounce) jigger vodka
- 1 (1.5 fluid ounce) jigger butterscotch schnapps
- 1 (1.5 fluid ounce) jigger Irish cream liqueur
- 1 (1.5 fluid ounce) jigger coffee flavored liqueur

DIRECTIONS

1. Fill a cocktail shaker with ice. Pour in the vodka, Irish cream, butterscotch schnapps and coffee liqueur. Shake well. Strain into shot glasses and serve.

ESPRESSO MARTINI

Servings: 2 | Prep: 5m | Cooks: 0m | Total: 5m

INGREDIENTS

- 1 fluid ounce vanilla flavored vodka
- 2 fluid ounces coffee-flavored liqueur
- 1 fluid ounce cream or milk
- 1 cup crushed ice

DIRECTIONS

1. Combine vodka, coffee liqueur, cream, and crushed ice in a cocktail shaker. Shake vigorously to chill. Pour into martini glasses, and serve.

POMACELLO MARTINI

Servings: 1 | Prep: 5m | Cooks: 0m | Total: 5m

NUTRITION FACTS

Calories: 261 | Carbohydrates: 29.1g | Fat: 0.1g | Protein: 0.2g | Cholesterol: 0mg

INGREDIENTS

- 3 fluid ounces pomegranate juice
- 1 1/2 fluid ounces vodka
- 1 fluid ounce limoncello liqueur
- 1 slice fresh lemon

DIRECTIONS

1. Pour the pomegranate juice, limoncello, and vodka into a cocktail shaker over ice. Cover and shake. Strain into a chilled martini glass, and garnish with a slice of lemon.

NIKKI'S SPECIAL CHOCOLATE MARTINI

Servings: 1 | Prep: 5m | Cooks: 0m | Total: 5m

INGREDIENTS

- 1 (1.5 fluid ounce) jigger chocolate liqueur
- 2 1/2 fluid ounces non-dairy vanilla-flavored creamer
- 1 (1.5 fluid ounce) jigger creme de cacao
- 2 teaspoons chocolate syrup
- 1 tablespoon vodka

DIRECTIONS

1. Pour the chocolate liqueur, creme de cacao, vodka, and creamer into a cocktail shaker over ice. Cover, and shake until the outside of the shaker has frosted. Dip the rim of a chilled martini glass in chocolate syrup. Strain the cocktail into the glass to serve.

PEPPERMINT MARTINI
Servings: 2 | Prep: 10m | Cooks: 0m | Total: 10m

NUTRITION FACTS

Calories: 325 | Carbohydrates: 17.4g | Fat: 0.1g | Protein: 0g | Cholesterol: 0mg

INGREDIENTS

- 5 fluid ounces vanilla-flavored vodka (such as Stoli)
- 2 fluid ounces white creme de menthe
- 1/2 fluid ounce peppermint schnapps

DIRECTIONS

1. Fill a cocktail shake with ice. Pour vodka, creme de menthe, and peppermint schnapps over the ice. Cover cocktail shaker and shake; strain into a martini glass.

WHITE RUSSIAN COCKTAIL
Servings: 1 | Prep: 5m | Cooks: 0m | Total: 5m

NUTRITION FACTS

Calories: 338 | Carbohydrates: 12g | Fat: 11.1g | Protein: 0.6g | Cholesterol: 41mg

INGREDIENTS

- 2 fluid ounces vodka
- 1 cup ice
- 1 fluid ounce coffee-flavored liqueur
- 1 fluid ounce heavy cream

DIRECTIONS

1. Combine vodka, coffee liqueur, and ice in an old-fashioned glass. Pour in cream.

WHISKEY PARALYZER
Servings: 1 | Prep: 5m | Cooks: 0m | Total: 5m

INGREDIENTS

- 1 cup ice cubes
- 1/2 cup root beer
- 1 fluid ounce Canadian whiskey, such as Crown Roya
- 2 fluid ounces milk
- 1 fluid ounce Kahlua or other coffee flavored liqueur

DIRECTIONS

1. Fill a highball glass with ice. Pour in the Canadian whiskey, coffee liqueur and root beer. Slowly pour in the milk so it does not curdle. Stir gently and enjoy immediately.

ROB AND BECKY'S PIMM LEMONADE

Servings: 6 | Prep: 15m | Cooks: 0m | Total: 15m

INGREDIENTS

- 1 cup Pimm's No. 1 (gin-based liqueur)
- 1/2 lemon, sliced
- 2 quarts lemonade
- 1/2 lime, sliced
- 1 (4 inch) wedge of cucumber
- 2 slices fresh pineapple (optional)
- 1 red apple, cored and thinly sliced
- 2 strawberries, sliced (optional)
- 1 orange, sliced
- 3 leaves fresh mint

DIRECTIONS

1. Stir together the Pimm's liqueur and lemonade together in a serving pitcher. Add the cucumber wedge, apple, orange, lemon, lime, pineapple, strawberries, and mint. Refrigerate until cold, or serve over ice.

COCOJITO (FROZEN MOJITO)

Servings: 2 | Prep: 10m | Cooks: 0m | Total: 10m

NUTRITION FACTS

Calories: 286 | Carbohydrates: 74.8g | Fat: 20.1g | Protein: 2.4g | Cholesterol: 0mg

INGREDIENTS

- 4 cups ice cubes
- 5 sprigs fresh mint leaves
- 2 1/2 limes, rind removed
- 2 mint sprigs, for garnish (optional)
- 7 fluid ounces sweetened cream of coconut (such as Coco Lopez)
- 2 lime wedges, for garnish (optional)
- 2 1/2 (1.5 fluid ounce) jiggers white rum (such as Bacardi)

DIRECTIONS

1. Blend the ice, limes, cream of coconut, rum, and mint leaves together in a blender until smooth. Pour into two glasses and garnish each with a mint sprig and lime wedge as desired.

SCORPION BOWL

Servings: 4 | Prep: 10m | Cooks: 0m | Total: 10m

INGREDIENTS

- 3 cups crushed ice
- 2 fluid ounces grenadine syrup
- 2 fluid ounces gin
- 8 fluid ounces fresh orange juice
- 1 fluid ounce dark rum
- 10 fluid ounces pineapple juice
- 2 fluid ounces 151 proof rum
- 3 fluid ounces fresh lemon juice (optional)
- 2 fluid ounces light rum
- 4 pineapple chunks
- 2 fluid ounces vodka
- 8 maraschino cherries

DIRECTIONS

1. Place the crushed ice in a large pitcher and pour in the gin, dark rum, 151 proof rum, light rum, vodka, grenadine, orange juice, pineapple juice, and lemon juice. Stir well to mix, then pour into a large, decorative cocktail glass and garnish with pineapple, cherries, and straws.

SIDECAR

Servings: 1 | Prep: 5m | Cooks: 0m | Total: 5m

INGREDIENTS

- ice cubes
- 1 fluid ounce brandy
- 1/2 fluid ounce freshly squeezed lemon juice
- 1 lemon wedge
- 1/2 fluid ounce Cointreau or triple sec

DIRECTIONS

1. Fill a cocktail shaker 3/4 full with ice cubes. Pour in lemon juice, Cointreau, and brandy. Cover and shake vigorously for about 30 seconds until the outside of the shaker becomes cold and frosty. Strain into a martini glass and garnish with a wedge of lemon.

ANNEX THEATER CHAMPAGNE COCKTAIL

Servings: 1 | Prep: 5m | Cooks: 0m | Total: 5m

INGREDIENTS

- 1 sugar cube
- 1 dash bitters (such as Angostura)
- 5 fluid ounces Champagne

DIRECTIONS

1. Place the sugar cube into a Champagne flute, and drop the bitters onto the sugar. Fill the flute with Champagne, and serve. Do not stir.

BEER MARGARITA

Servings: 6 | Prep: 2m | Cooks: 0m | Total: 2m

INGREDIENTS

- 1 (6 ounce) can frozen lemonade concentrate
- 8 fluid ounces vodka
- 3 (12 fluid ounce) cans or bottles beer

DIRECTIONS

1. Empty lemonade concentrate into pitcher (do not add water!). Pour in vodka and beer. Serve over ice.

RED SNAPPER

Servings: 1 | Prep: 1m | Cooks: 0m | Total: 1m

INGREDIENTS

- 1 (1.5 fluid ounce) jigger deluxe Canadian whiskey
- 1 (1.5 fluid ounce) jigger amaretto liqueur
- 4 fluid ounces cranberry juice

DIRECTIONS

1. Fill a tall glass with ice. Pour in the whiskey and amaretto, then fill to the top with cranberry juice. Stir and enjoy.

CHERRY VODKA SOUR

Servings: 1 | Prep: 5m | Cooks: 0m | Total: 5m

INGREDIENTS

- 3 fluid ounces vodka
- 3 fluid ounces sweet and sour mix
- 1 tablespoon cherry grenadine syrup

DIRECTIONS

1. Stir together vodka, sweet and sour mix, and grenadine in an 8 ounce glass. Fill with ice.

STORM OF THE CENTURY HURRICANE

Servings: 1 | Prep: 2m | Cooks: 0m | Total: 2m

INGREDIENTS

- 1 cup ice cubes
- 1 fluid ounce Chambord (raspberry liqueur)
- 1 fluid ounce light rum
- 1 fluid ounce triple sec liqueur
- 1 fluid ounce dark rum
- 3 fluid ounces orange juice
- 1 fluid ounce coconut rum
- orange slices for garnish (optional)
- 1 fluid ounce vodka
- maraschino cherry for garnish (optional)
- 1 fluid ounce gin

DIRECTIONS

1. Fill a hurricane glass with ice. Add light rum, dark rum, coconut rum, vodka, gin, raspberry liqueur, triple sec and orange juice. Shake gently, and garnish with orange slices and a cherry, if desired. Beverage will be about the color of a pink grapefruit.

BASIC BLOODY MARY

Servings: 1 | Prep: 2m | Cooks: 0m | Total: 2m

INGREDIENTS

- 1 (11.5 ounce) can tomato-vegetable juice cocktail
- 1/3 cup vodka

DIRECTIONS

1. In a large glass over ice, pour 1/2 can of tomato-vegetable juice cocktail. Stir in the vodka.

CHOCOLATE MINT SHOT

Servings: 1 | Prep: 1m | Cooks: 0m | Total: 1m

INGREDIENTS

- 3/4 fluid ounce Irish cream liqueur
- 1/2 fluid ounce white chocolate liqueur
- 1/4 fluid ounce creme de menthe liqueur

DIRECTIONS

1. Fill a shot glass half-full with Irish cream. Pour in chocolate liqueur to three-fourths full. Top with creme de menthe.

KEY LIME PIE

Servings: 2 | Prep: 5m | Cooks: 0m | Total: 5m

INGREDIENTS

- 1/2 lime, cut into wedges
- 1 teaspoon vanilla extract
- 4 fluid ounces vodka
- 2 twists lime zest, garnish
- 1 1/2 fluid ounces frozen limeade concentrate, thawed

DIRECTIONS

1. Place the lime wedges in the bottom of a mixing glass and muddle them well. Cover with ice, and pour in vodka, lime juice, and vanilla. Shake well, then strain into two stemmed cocktail glasses. Garnish each with a twist of lime.

PINEAPPLE BREEZE

Servings: 1 | Prep: 5m | Cooks: 0m | Total: 5m

NUTRITION FACTS

Calories: 288 | Carbohydrates: 49.5g | Fat: 0.2g | Protein: 0.7g | Cholesterol: 0mg

INGREDIENTS

- 1 1/2 cups ice cubes
- 2 fluid ounces pineapple juice, or to taste
- 2 (1.5 fluid ounce) jiggers coconut-flavored rum (such as Malibu)
- 2 fluid ounces orange juice, or to taste
- 1/2 (12 ounce) can lemon-lime soda (such as Sprite)

DIRECTIONS

1. Place the ice into a 16-ounce glass. Pour in the rum, lemon-lime soda, pineapple juice, and orange juice. Stir and serve.

TOP SHELF MARGARITAS ON THE ROCKS

Servings: 16 | Prep: 10m | Cooks: 0m | Total: 10m

INGREDIENTS

- 2/3 cup sugar
- 2 cups ice cubes
- 1/3 cup water
- 2 cups premium tequila
- 2 1/4 cups water
- 1 cup Cointreau
- 1 1/2 cups fresh lemon juice
- 1/2 cup lime juice
- 1/4 cup sugar
- 16 lime wedges
- 1 egg white
- coarse kosher salt

DIRECTIONS

1. Make a simple syrup by stirring together and bringing 2/3 cup sugar and 1/3 cup water to a boil until the sugar dissolves; set aside to cool.
2. Make the sour mix by briskly stirring together the 2 1/4 cups water, lemon juice, 1/4 cup sugar, and egg white; set aside.
3. Combine the ice cubes, tequila, Cointreau, lime juice, 1 ounce of the simple syrup, and 1/2 cup of the sour mix in a pitcher; stir vigorously to infuse the ice, 8 to 15 seconds.
4. Run a lime wedge along the rim of an 8-ounce glass. Spread the kosher salt onto a plate and dip the glass rims in the salt to coat; add ice if desired. Strain the mixture from the cocktail shaker into the glass to serve.

TOM COLLINS

Servings: 1 | Prep: 5m | Cooks: 0m | Total: 5m

INGREDIENTS

- 2 fluid ounces gin
- 1 cup ice cubes
- 2 fluid ounces lemon juice
- 1/4 cup cold club soda
- 1 fluid ounce simple syrup
- 1 slice lemon, for garnish
- 1 dash bitters
- 1 maraschino cherry

DIRECTIONS

1. Fill a cocktail shaker with ice. Pour in the gin, lemon juice, simple syrup and a dash of bitters. Cover and shake until the outside of the container is frosty, about 15 seconds. Strain into a highball glass full of ice. Top off with club soda and garnish with a lemon slice and maraschino cherry.

MEYER LEMON MARTINI

Servings: 1 | Prep: 10m | Cooks: 0m | Total: 10m

INGREDIENTS

- 2 teaspoons white sugar
- 1 fluid ounce orange-flavored liqueur (such as Cointreau)
- 2 teaspoons warm water
- ice
- 1 Meyer lemon, juiced and peeled
- 1 teaspoon white sugar, or as needed for rimming
- 2 fluid ounces vodka

DIRECTIONS

1. Combine 2 teaspoons sugar and warm water in a cocktail shaker; stir to dissolve sugar. Pour Meyer lemon juice, lemon peels, vodka, and orange liqueur into the shaker; add ice. Cover and shake vigorously.
2. Remove a lemon peel from the shaker and wipe the rim of a martini glass with the peel. Dip the rim of the glass in 1 teaspoon sugar, or as needed. Strain martini into prepared glass.

RUBY RED GRAPEFRUIT MARTINI

Servings: 1 | Prep: 10m | Cooks: 0m | Total: 10m

NUTRITION FACTS

Calories: 241 | Carbohydrates: 31.1g | Fat: 0.1g | Protein: 0.3g | Cholesterol: 0mg

INGREDIENTS

- 1 tablespoon white sugar
- 1 fluid ounce vodka
- 1 cup ice, or as needed
- 1 fluid ounce triple sec
- 2 fluid ounces Ruby red grapefruit juice

DIRECTIONS

1. Pour sugar onto a small plate. Wet the rim of a martini glass with cold water; dip rim in the sugar to coat.
2. Fill cocktail shaker with ice; pour in grapefruit juice, vodka, and triple sec. Cover shaker with lid and shake. Strain and pour mixture into prepared martini glass.

STRAWBERRY SHORTCAKE DRINK

Servings: 1 | Prep: 5m | Cooks: 0m | Total: 5m

NUTRITION FACTS

Calories: 476 | Carbohydrates: 55.4g | Fat: 17.5g | Protein: 5.2g | Cholesterol: 68mg

INGREDIENTS

- 1/4 cup frozen strawberries, thawed
- 1/2 cup crushed ice
- 1 1/4 fluid ounces amaretto liqueur
- 1/4 fluid ounce vanilla-flavored vodka (optional)
- 2 (1/2 cup) scoops vanilla ice cream

- 1 tablespoon whipped cream
- 1 dash vanilla extract
- 1 fresh strawberry

DIRECTIONS

1. Place thawed frozen strawberries, amaretto liqueur, vanilla ice cream, vanilla extract, crushed ice, and vanilla vodka into a blender.
2. Cover and blend until smooth.
3. Pour into a glass and garnish with whipped cream and a fresh strawberry.

BAYBREEZE COCKTAIL

Servings: 1 | Prep: 5m | Cooks: 0m | Total: 5m

NUTRITION FACTS

Calories: 184 | Carbohydrates: 23.7g | Fat: 0.3g | Protein: 0.7g | Cholesterol: 0mg

INGREDIENTS

- 1 cup ice
- 1 1/2 fluid ounces vodka
- 2 fluid ounces cranberry juice
- 1 lime wedge for garnish
- 2 fluid ounces pineapple juice

DIRECTIONS

1. Combine ice, cranberry juice, pineapple juice, and vodka in a highball glass. Garnish with a lime wedge.

SICILIAN SUNSET

Servings: 4 | Prep: 10m | Cooks: 0m | Total: 10m

NUTRITION FACTS

Calories: 115 | Carbohydrates: 17.2g | Fat: 0.2g | Protein: 0.5g | Cholesterol: 0mg

INGREDIENTS

- 2 cups ice cubes
- 1 cup cranberry juice
- 1 cup Prosecco (Italian sparkling wine)
- 2 lemons, zested

- 1 cup orange juice

DIRECTIONS

1. Place the ice in a glass pitcher. Pour in the Prosecco, orange juice, and cranberry juice; stir. Pour the cocktail into champagne flutes, and sprinkle with lemon zest to serve.

NEXT BEST THING TO LULU'S PINA COLADA

Servings: 4 | Prep: 10m | Cooks: 0m | Total: 10m

NUTRITION FACTS

Calories: 640 | Carbohydrates: 34.6g | Fat: 10.6g | Protein: 2.1g | Cholesterol: 35mg

INGREDIENTS

- 1 (10 ounce) can frozen pina colada mix
- 8 cubes ice
- 1 cup crushed pineapple in juice, undrained
- 1/4 cup whipping cream
- 1 cup vanilla ice cream
- 4 cherries with stems
- 1 (750 milliliter) bottle mango flavored rum

DIRECTIONS

1. Combine the pina colada mix, pineapple with juice, vanilla ice cream, rum, and ice in a blender. Blend until slushy.
2. Pour the whipping cream into a bowl, and beat until soft peaks form. Stir into the pina colada mixture to blend evenly; pour into four glasses. Top each drink with a cherry.

LYNCHBURG LEMONADE

Servings: 1 | Prep: 5m | Cooks: 0 | Total: 5m

INGREDIENTS

- 1 cup ice cubes
- 1 (1.5 fluid ounce) jigger triple sec (orange-flavored liqueur)
- 1 (1.5 fluid ounce) jigger Tennessee whiskey
- 3/4 cup chilled lemon-lime soda
- 1 (1.5 fluid ounce) jigger sweet and sour mix

DIRECTIONS

1. Fill a tall glass with ice cubes and pour in the whiskey, sweet and sour mix, triple sec and lemon-lime soda. Stir with a straw and enjoy.

VODKA COLLINS

Servings: 1 | Prep: 10m | Cooks: 0m | Total: 10m

INGREDIENTS

- 1 1/2 fluid ounces vodka
- 1 slice orange, garnish
- 3 fluid ounces sweet and sour mix
- 1 maraschino cherry, garnish
- 1 cup carbonated water
- ice

DIRECTIONS

1. In a cocktail shaker filled with ice, combine vodka and sweet and sour. Shake well, then strain into a tall glass full of ice. Fill the glass with carbonated water. Cut orange slice into quarters.
2. On a cocktail sword, spear cherry first, then spear orange slice through the peel. Hang sword from the rim of the glass, so that fruit is in the drink.

LIME-AID

Servings: 4 | Prep: 6m | Cooks: 0m | Total: 6m

INGREDIENTS

- 1 (6 ounce) can frozen limeade concentrate
- 3 fluid ounces vodka
- 1 tray ice cubes
- 1 lime, sliced
- 3 fluid ounces water

DIRECTIONS

1. In a blender, combine limeade concentrate, ice cubes, water and vodka. Blend until smooth. Pour into 6 ounce stem glasses, and garnish with lime slices.

STRAWBERRY MARGARITA

Servings: 4 | Prep: 5m | Cooks: 0m | Total: 5m

NUTRITION FACTS

Calories: 311 | Carbohydrates: 39.1g | Fat: 0.2g | Protein: 0.5g | Cholesterol: 0mg

INGREDIENTS

- 1 (10 ounce) package frozen strawberries
- 1/4 cup triple sec
- 1 (6 ounce) can frozen pink lemonade concentrate
- ice cubes
- 1 cup tequila

DIRECTIONS

1. Place strawberries, lemonade concentrate, tequila, and triple sec in a blender. Blend until smooth. Add ice cubes as needed.

STRIP AND GO NAKED

Servings: 55 | Prep: 10m | Cooks: 1m | Total: 11m

INGREDIENTS

- 30 (12 fluid ounce) cans or bottles Keystone Light beer
- 1 3/4 liters vodka
- 2 (12 ounce) cans frozen lemonade concentrate, thawed

DIRECTIONS

1. In a 4 to 5 gallon sports drink dispenser, combine the light beer, vodka and lemonade concentrate. Stir gently to disperse the lemonade. Put the lid on and serve.

BLUE RITA

Servings: 1 | Prep: 1m | Cooks: 0m | Total: 1m

INGREDIENTS

- 1 1/4 fluid ounces tequila
- 4 fluid ounces sour mix
- 3/4 fluid ounce Blue Curacao
- 1 slice lime wedge
- 1/2 fluid ounce coconut rum

DIRECTIONS

1. In a cocktail mixer full of ice, combine tequila, Blue Curacao, coconut rum and sour mix. Shake vigorously and strain into glass. Garnish with a wedge of lime.

FROZEN LIME DAIQUIRI

Servings: 6 | Prep: 5m | Cooks: 0m | Total: 5m

INGREDIENTS

- 1 (12 fluid ounce) can frozen limeade concentrate
- 12 fluid ounces rum
- 1 tray ice cubes

DIRECTIONS

1. In a blender, combine limeade concentrate, rum and ice cubes. Blend until smooth. Pour into glasses and serve immediately.

KAMIKAZE

Servings: 1 | Prep: 5m | Cooks: 0m | Total: 5m

INGREDIENTS

- 2 (1.5 fluid ounce) jiggers vodka
- 1 (1.5 fluid ounce) jigger fresh lime juice
- 2 (1.5 fluid ounce) jiggers triple sec liqueur
- 1 (1.5 fluid ounce) jigger bottled lime juice

DIRECTIONS

1. In a cocktail shaker full of ice combine vodka, triple sec, fresh lime juice and bottled lime juice. Shake, don't stir and strain into a chilled glass.

PIRATE'S LAST CALL

Servings: 1 | Prep: 5m | Cooks: 0m | Total: 5m

INGREDIENTS

- 4 maraschino cherries
- 1 cup ice cubes
- 2 teaspoons white sugar
- 1 cup cherry vanilla carbonated cola
- 1 (1.5 fluid ounce) jigger rum (dark or light)

DIRECTIONS

1. Place the cherries and sugar in the bottom of a 12 ounce glass, and mash with a spoon or muddler. Add the rum and ice. Pour in the soda, stir, and serve.

TEXATINI

Servings: 1 | Prep: 15m | Cooks: 0m | Total: 15m

INGREDIENTS

- coarse salt (optional)
- 1 fluid ounce orange juice
- 1 (1.5 fluid ounce) jigger tequila
- 1 cup crushed ice
- 1 (1.5 fluid ounce) jigger orange liqueur (Cointreau, Triple Sec or Grand Marnier)
- 1 jalapeno-stuffed green olive
- 1/2 cup sweet and sour mix

DIRECTIONS

1. Slightly moisten rim of a large martini glass, and dip in course salt to rim the glass.
2. Combine tequila, orange liqueur, sweet and sour mix, orange juice, and ice in a shaker. Shake vigorously, and strain into martini glass. Garnish with jalapeno-stuffed green olives.

MADRAS COCKTAIL

Servings: 1 | Prep: 5m | Cooks: 0m | Total: 5m

NUTRITION FACTS

Calories: 180 | Carbohydrates: 20.8g | Fat: 0.2g | Protein: 0.3g | Cholesterol: 0mg

INGREDIENTS

- 1 1/2 fluid ounces vodka
- 1/2 cup ice
- 4 fluid ounces cranberry juice
- 1 lime wedge
- 1 fluid ounce orange juice

DIRECTIONS

1. Combine vodka, cranberry juice, and orange juice in a highball glass. Add ice and stir to combine. Garnish with a wedge of lime.

DILL PICKLE MARTINI

Servings: 2 | Prep: 5m | Cooks: 0m | Total: 5m

NUTRITION FACTS

Calories: 146 | Carbohydrates: 0.3g | Fat: 0g | Protein: 0g | Cholesterol: 0mg

INGREDIENTS

- 2 cups ice
- 4 1/2 fluid ounces vodka
- 1 1/2 fluid ounces dill pickle juice
- 2 dill pickle spears

DIRECTIONS

1. Pour ice into a cocktail shaker; pour dill pickle juice and vodka over the ice. Cover the shaker and shake vigorously for about 20 seconds; strain into martini glasses. Garnish each cocktail with a dill pickle spear.

MOJITO PERFECTO

Servings: 2 | Prep: 5m | Cooks: 0m | Total: 5m

NUTRITION FACTS

Calories: 139 | Carbohydrates: 11.9g | Fat: 0.1g | Protein: 0.2g | Cholesterol: 0mg

INGREDIENTS

- 6 mint leaves
- 2 (1.5 fluid ounce) jiggers lemon-flavored rum
- 4 teaspoons white sugar
- 1 cup ice cubes, or as needed
- 1 lime, cut into 6 wedges
- 1/2 cup carbonated water, or as needed

DIRECTIONS

1. Put 3 mint leaves and 2 teaspoons sugar into each of 2 glass tumblers; vigorously stir sugar and mint together, crushing mint with the back of a spoon to release oils. Add 3 lime wedges to each glass; again stir vigorously to release some lime juice. Pour 1 jigger rum into each glass. Fill glasses with ice cubes and top with carbonated water; stir.

DANI'S BUTT KICKIN' BLOODY MARY MIX

Servings: 8 | Prep: 10m | Cooks: 8h | Total: 8h10m

NUTRITION FACTS

Calories: 58 | Carbohydrates: 11.3g | Fat: 0.4g | Protein: 2.2g | Cholesterol: <1mg

INGREDIENTS

- 1 (46 fluid ounce) bottle tomato-vegetable juice cocktail
- 2 tablespoons lemon juice
- 1 (8 ounce) bottle clam juice
- 1 tablespoon brown sugar
- 6 tablespoons low-salt Worcestershire sauce
- 1 tablespoon concentrated beef base (paste)
- 6 tablespoons prepared horseradish
- 1 tablespoon celery salt
- 2 tablespoons hot pepper sauce (such as Tabasco)
- 1 teaspoon ground black pepper

DIRECTIONS

1. Mix vegetable juice cocktail, clam juice, Worcestershire sauce, horseradish, hot sauce, lemon juice, brown sugar, beef base, celery salt, and black pepper in a large pitcher, stirring until brown sugar and celery salt have dissolved. Allow to chill for at least 8 hours.

MINT-CUCUMBER MOJITOS

Servings: 1 | Prep: 15m | Cooks: 0m | Total: 15m

INGREDIENTS

- 1 lime, quartered
- 6 cubes ice, or as needed
- 2 sprigs fresh mint leaves
- 2 ounces white rum (such as Bacardi)
- 1 tablespoon white sugar
- 4 fluid ounces club soda
- 2 slices cucumber

DIRECTIONS

1. Squeeze the lime quarters into a highball glass, and drop the limes into the glass. Add the mint leaves and sugar. Muddle well with the back of a spoon or with a muddler. Place the cucumber slices

into the glass, and fill with ice cubes. Pour in the rum, then top off with club soda. Stir gently and serve.

POMEGRANATE MARGARITA

Servings: 6 | Prep: 15m | Cooks: 0m | Total: 15m

INGREDIENTS

- 1 cup tequila
- 4 cups ice
- 1 cup triple sec
- 1 cup pomegranate juice
- 1/4 cup confectioners' sugar
- 1 cup fresh lime juice

DIRECTIONS

1. Pour the tequila and triple sec into a pitcher. Sprinkle in the confectioners' sugar, and stir to dissolve. Add the ice, and pour in the pomegranate juice and lime juice. Stir to mix, then serve. You can add more tequila to taste if you're a professional.

RYE MANHATTAN

Servings: 1 | Prep: 5m | Cooks: 0m | Total: 5m

INGREDIENTS

- 1/4 cup rye whiskey
- 2 dashes Angostura bitters
- 2 tablespoons sweet vermouth
- 1 maraschino cherry

DIRECTIONS

1. Fill a cocktail shaker with ice cubes. Pour in the whiskey, vermouth and bitters. Shake until frosty, about 15 seconds then strain into a Manhattan glass and garnish with a maraschino cherry.

WORLD'S BEST BLOODY MARY MIX

Servings: 8 | Prep: 10m | Cooks: 0m | Total: 10m

NUTRITION FACTS

Calories: 50 | Carbohydrates: 12.8g | Fat: 0.3g | Protein: 1.7g | Cholesterol: 0mg

INGREDIENTS

- 1 (46 fluid ounce) can tomato juice
- 1 teaspoon ground black pepper
- 1/3 cup steak sauce
- 1 pinch cayenne pepper, or to taste
- 3 tablespoons hickory smoke-flavored barbeque sauce
- 8 wedges lemon, divided (optional)
- 1 teaspoon ground celery seed
- 8 celery sticks, divided (optional)
- 1 teaspoon garlic salt

DIRECTIONS

1. Stir tomato juice, steak sauce, barbeque sauce, celery seed, garlic salt, and black pepper in a large pitcher. Serve in glasses over ice and garnish each serving with a pinch of cayenne pepper, a lemon wedge, and a celery stick.

MANHATTAN COCKTAIL

Servings: 1 | Prep: 5m | Cooks: 0m | Total: 5m

NUTRITION FACTS

Calories: 169 | Carbohydrates: 4g | Fat: 0g | Protein: 0g | Cholesterol: 0mg

INGREDIENTS

- 2 fluid ounces rye whiskey
- 1 cup ice cubes
- 1/2 fluid ounce sweet vermouth
- 1 maraschino cherry
- 1 dash Angostura bitters

DIRECTIONS

1. Combine whiskey, vermouth, and bitters in a cocktail mixing class. Add ice and stir until chilled. Strain into a chilled cocktail glass.
2. Garnish with a maraschino cherry.

OLD FASHIONED COCKTAIL

Servings: 1 | Prep: 5m | Cooks: 0m | Total: 5m

NUTRITION FACTS

INGREDIENTS

- sugar cube
- 1 lemon twist
- 1 teaspoon water
- ice cubes
- 1 dash bitters
- 1 orange slice, for garnish
- 2 fluid ounces whiskey (rye or bourbon)
- 1 maraschino cherry, for garnish

DIRECTIONS

1. Muddle sugar cube, water, and bitters in an old fashioned glass for 1 minute. Pour in whiskey and stir for an additional minute. Squeeze the lemon twist over the glass and drop it in. Add ice cubes. Garnish with a slice of orange and a maraschino cherry; serve with a swizzle stick.

CREAMY COCONUT MARGARITA

Servings: 6 | Prep: 10m | Cooks: 0m | Total: 10m

NUTRITION FACTS

Calories: 379 | Carbohydrates: 48.4g | Fat: 12.6g | Protein: 0.1g | Cholesterol: 0mg

INGREDIENTS

- 1 (15 ounce) can cream of coconut (such as Coco Lopez)
- 1/2 cup freshly squeezed lime juice
- 1 cup ice
- 1/4 cup brandy-based orange liqueur (such as Grand Marnier)
- 3/4 cup tequila (such as Sauza® 100% Blue Agave)

DIRECTIONS

1. Blend cream of coconut, ice, tequila, lime juice, and orange liqueur in a blender until smooth.

KETO MARGARITA

Servings: 1 | Prep: 10m | Cooks: 0m | Total: 10m

INGREDIENTS

- 3 cups ice

- 1 tablespoon coarse salt
- 2 fluid ounces tequila
- 2 lime wedges
- 1 fluid ounce lime juice
- 1 pint-sized Mason jar
- 2 1/2 teaspoons low-calorie natural sweetener (such as Swerve)
- 2 fluid ounces orange-flavored sparkling water (such as La Croix)

DIRECTIONS

1. Fill a shaker half-full with ice. Add tequila, lime juice, and sweetener to the shaker. Seal and shake vigorously until outside is frosted, 10 to 15 seconds.
2. Place salt on a plate. Run 1 lime wedge along the rim of the Mason jar. Press the jar down into the salt. Fill the jar with ice cubes.
3. Strain margarita into the jar. Top with sparkling water and stir. Garnish with remaining lime wedge.

GERRY'S MARGARITA

Servings: 1 | Prep: 10m | Cooks: 0m | Total: 10m

NUTRITION FACTS

Calories: 322 | Carbohydrates: 32.2g | Fat: 0g | Protein: 0.2g | Cholesterol: 0mg

INGREDIENTS

- 1 lime, juiced
- 1 cup ice cubes, or as needed
- 1/2 lemon, juiced
- salt as needed
- 2 tablespoons white sugar
- 1 teaspoon brandy-based orange liqueur (such as Grand Marnier), or to taste (optional)
- 2 (1.5 fluid ounce) jiggers reposado tequila (such as Jose Cuervo® Gold)

DIRECTIONS

1. Squeeze lime juice and lemon juice into a cocktail shaker; top with sugar. Pour tequila over sugar mixture and add ice. Cover shaker and shake. Allow shaker to rest for 1 to 2 minutes.
2. Spread salt onto a plate. Rub the lemon around the rim of the margarita glass and dip the rim into the salt to coat. Pour margarita into glass and top with brandy-based orange liqueur.

TOM COLLINS COCKTAIL

Servings: 1 | Prep: 5m | Cooks: 0m | Total: 5m

NUTRITION FACTS

Calories: 191 | Carbohydrates: 12.8g | Fat: 0g | Protein: 0.2g | Cholesterol: 0mg

INGREDIENTS

- 1 1/2 cups ice
- 1 cup ice
- 2 fluid ounces gin
- 2 fluid ounces club soda
- 3/4 fluid ounce lemon juice
- 1 lemon wedge
- 1/2 fluid ounce simple syrup

DIRECTIONS

1. Fill a Collins glass with 1 1/2 cups ice, set aside in the freezer. Combine gin, lemon juice, and simple syrup in a cocktail shaker. Add 1 cup ice, cover and shake until chilled. Strain into the chilled Collins glass.
2. Top with club soda and garnish with a lemon wedge.

CHOCOLATE MARTINI COCKTAIL

Servings: 1 | Prep: 5m | Cooks: 0m | Total: 5m

NUTRITION FACTS

Calories: 511 | Carbohydrates: 50.9g | Fat: 9g | Protein: 2.2g | Cholesterol: 28mg

INGREDIENTS

- 1 1/2 fluid ounces chocolate liqueur
- 2 1/2 fluid ounces half-and-half
- 1 1/2 fluid ounces creme de cacao
- 1 cup ice
- 1/2 fluid ounce vodka

DIRECTIONS

1. Combine chocolate liqueur, creme de cacao, vodka, half-and-half, and ice in a cocktail shaker. Cover and shake until chilled. Strain into a chilled cocktail glass.

POMEGRANATE MARTINI

Servings: 2 | Prep: 5m | Cooks: 0m | Total: 5m

INGREDIENTS

- 4 fluid ounces pomegranate juice
- 2 fluid ounces orange-flavored liqueur
- 2 fluid ounces cranberry juice cocktail
- 1 fluid ounce grenadine syrup
- 2 fluid ounces raspberry vodka
- 1 cup crushed ice

DIRECTIONS

1. Combine pomegranate juice, cranberry juice, raspberry vodka, orange-flavored liqueur, grenadine syrup, and crushed ice in a shaker. Shake vigorously to chill. Pour into martini glasses, and serve.

CHOCOLATE COVERED CHERRY MARTINI

Servings: 1 | Prep: 5m | Cooks: 0m | Total: 5m

NUTRITION FACTS

Calories: 444 | Carbohydrates: 34.9g | Fat: 5.1g | Protein: 1.2g | Cholesterol: 12mg

INGREDIENTS

- 1 cup ice cubes
- 1 fluid ounce half-and-half
- 1 (1.5 fluid ounce) jigger chocolate vodka
- 1 dash chocolate syrup
- 1 (1.5 fluid ounce) jigger cherry vodka
- 1 maraschino cherry
- 1/2 fluid ounce grenadine syrup
- 1 chocolate kiss candy
- 1 fluid ounce creme de cacao

DIRECTIONS

1. Fill a cocktail shaker with ice cubes. Pour in chocolate and cherry vodkas, grenadine, creme de cacao, half-and-half, and chocolate syrup. Cover and shake until the outside of the shaker has frosted. Strain into a chilled martini glass, garnish with maraschino cherry and chocolate kiss, and serve.

VODKA PARALYZER

Servings: 1 | Prep: 5m | Cooks: 0m | Total: 5m

INGREDIENTS

- 1 cup ice cubes
- 1 (1.5 fluid ounce) jigger vodka
- 4 fluid ounces cola
- 2 fluid ounces milk
- 1 fluid ounce coffee flavored liqueur
- 1 maraschino cherry (optional)

DIRECTIONS

1. Fill a highball glass with ice. Pour in the cola, coffee liqueur, vodka, and milk. Stir briefly and top with a cherry.

CARAMEL LIQUEUR

Servings: 32 | Prep: 5m | Cooks: 4h | Total: 4h40m

INGREDIENTS

- 2 (14 ounce) cans sweetened condensed milk
- 1 1/4 cups spiced rum

DIRECTIONS

1. Remove the labels from the cans of milk. Place the cans into a large saucepan, and cover with a few inches of water. Bring to a boil over high heat, then reduce heat to medium, cover, and simmer for 4 hours. Keep an eye on the water level, and add water as needed to keep at least an inch of water above the cans. After the cans have boiled for 4 hours, remove from the boiling water and set aside to cool for 35 minutes.
2. Open the cans and scrape the browned milk into a bowl, whisk in the spiced rum until smooth, then pour into a bottle with a top. The liqueur will keep for several months in the refrigerator.

THE ULTIMATE SHAKEN BLOODY MARY

Servings: 2 | Prep: 10m | Cooks: 0m | Total: 10m

INGREDIENTS

- 2 (12 fluid ounce) cans tomato juice
- 1/2 teaspoon celery salt
- 1/4 teaspoon hot sauce such as Tabasco
- 1/2 cup vodka
- 1 teaspoon Worcestershire sauce
- 4 cornichons (small dill pickles)
- 1 teaspoon dill weed
- 2 cups ice cubes

- 1 tablespoon seafood seasoning, such as Old Bay

DIRECTIONS

1. Pour the tomato juice, hot sauce, Worcestershire sauce, dill, seafood seasoning, celery salt, and vodka into a cocktail shaker over ice. Cover, and shake until the outside of the shaker has frosted. Strain into ice-filled glasses, and garnish with cornichons to serve.

WHITE CHRISTMAS COCKTAIL
Servings: 2 | Prep: 5m | Cooks: 0m | Total: 5m

NUTRITION FACTS

Calories: 184 | Carbohydrates: 15.7g | Fat: 5.6g | Protein: 0.3g | Cholesterol: 20mg

INGREDIENTS

- 1 fluid ounce heavy cream
- 1 fluid ounce white creme de cacao
- 1 fluid ounce vodka
- 1 cup ice cubes
- 1 fluid ounce peppermint schnapps
- 1 small candy cane (optional)

DIRECTIONS

1. Pour the heavy cream, vodka, schnapps, and white creme de cacao into a cocktail shaker over ice. Cover, and shake until the outside of the shaker has frosted. Strain into a chilled glass, and garnish with a mini candy cane to serve.

CRANTINI
Servings: 1 | Prep: 1m | Cooks: 0m | Total: 1m

INGREDIENTS

- 1 fluid ounce vodka
- 4 fluid ounces lemon-lime flavored carbonated beverage
- 3 fluid ounces cranberry juice
- 1 lemon - cut into wedges, for garnish

DIRECTIONS

1. Pour cranberry juice and vodka into a cocktail shaker full of ice. Strain into your serving glass. Add lemon-lime soda and stir. Squeeze a lemon wedge into glass and stir again.

DIRTY GIRL SCOUT

Servings: 1 | Prep: 5m | Cooks: 0m | Total: 5m

INGREDIENTS

- 1 fluid ounce vodka
- 1 fluid ounce Irish cream liqueur
- 1 fluid ounce coffee liqueur
- 1 mint leaf
- 1 fluid ounce creme de menthe

DIRECTIONS

1. Pour the vodka, coffee liqueur, creme de menthe, and Irish cream into a cocktail shaker over ice. Cover, and shake until the outside of the shaker has frosted. Strain into a chilled martini glass and garnish with a mint leaf to serve.

SCARLET KISS

Servings: 1 | Prep: 1m | Cooks: 0m | Total: 1m

INGREDIENTS

- 1 (1.5 fluid ounce) jigger raspberry vodka
- 1 (1.5 fluid ounce) jigger Chambord (raspberry liqueur)
- 1 (1.5 fluid ounce) jigger strawberry vodka
- 1 twist orange zest
- 1 fluid ounce lemon-lime flavored carbonated beverage

DIRECTIONS

1. In an old-fashioned glass over ice, combine raspberry vodka, strawberry vodka, and lemon-lime soda. Float raspberry liqueur on top. garnish with a twist of orange zest.

CLASSIC FROZEN STRAWBERRY MARGARITA

Servings: 1 | Prep: 10m | Cooks: 0m | Total: 10m

NUTRITION FACTS

Calories: 206 | Carbohydrates: 21.3g | Fat: 0.2g | Protein: 0.4g | Cholesterol: 0mg

INGREDIENTS

- 1/4 cup sliced fresh strawberries

- 1 teaspoon white sugar, or to taste
- 1 1/2 fluid ounces tequila
- 1 cup ice cubes
- 1 fluid ounce lime juice
- 1 wedge lime (optional)
- 1/2 fluid ounce triple sec
- 1 teaspoon white sugar (optional)

DIRECTIONS

1. Blend strawberries, tequila, lime juice, triple sec, and 1 teaspoon sugar in blender to combine, about 10 seconds. Add ice cubes; blend on high until the ice is crushed, about 15 seconds.
2. Rub lime wedge around the rim of a glass. Spread 1 teaspoon sugar onto a plate. Dip glass rim in sugar to coat. Pour margarita into the glass.

ORANGE CRUSH! FRESH SQUEEZED ORANGE AND VODKA COCKTAIL

Servings: 1 | Prep: 10m | Cooks: 0m | Total: 10m

NUTRITION FACTS

Calories: 325 | Carbohydrates: 34.7g | Fat: 0.4g | Protein: 1.3g | Cholesterol: 0mg

INGREDIENTS

- 2 cups ice cubes, or as needed
- 2 Valencia oranges, juiced
- 2 fluid ounces orange-flavored vodka
- 1 splash lemon-lime soda (such as Sprite) (optional)
- 1 fluid ounce triple sec liqueur
- 1 slice orange

DIRECTIONS

1. Fill a pint glass with ice cubes. Pour orange-flavored vodka, triple sec, and orange juice over ice; top with lemon-lime soda. Mix well and garnish with orange slice.

BEAST MODE VODKA

Servings: 8 | Prep: 5m | Cooks: 0m | Total: 5m

NUTRITION FACTS

Calories: 148 | Carbohydrates: 11.6g | Fat: 0.6g | Protein: 0g | Cholesterol: 0mg

INGREDIENTS

- 12 fluid ounces vodka
- 1/2 cup blue or green fruit-flavored candies (such as Skittles)

DIRECTIONS

1. Combine vodka and candies in a jar with a lid or cocktail shaker. Cover and shake until the colored candy coating has dissolved, about 10 seconds. Strain into a resealable bottle.

HALLOWEEN CANDY CORN JELL-O SHOTS
Servings: 16 | Prep: 15m | Cooks: 3h30m | Total: 3h45m

NUTRITION FACTS

Calories: 202 | Carbohydrates: 22.4g | Fat: 2.1g | Protein: 3.3g | Cholesterol: 8mg

INGREDIENTS

- 1 1/2 cups boiling water, divided
- 2 tablespoons warm water
- 1 (3 ounce) package lemon-flavored gelatin mix (such as Jell-O)
- 1 (.25 ounce) envelope unflavored gelatin
- 2 cups vodka, divided
- 1 (14 ounce) can sweetened condensed milk
- ice cubes
- 1/2 cup light rum
- 1 (3 ounce) package orange-flavored gelatin mix (such as Jell-O)

DIRECTIONS

1. Pour 3/4 cup boiling water into a small bowl. Add lemon gelatin mix; stir until dissolved. Pour 1 cup vodka into a glass measuring cup; add enough ice to make 1 1/4 cup. Stir into lemon gelatin until slightly thickened; remove any unmelted ice. Fill tall shot glasses 1/3 of the way with lemon gelatin mixture.
2. Refrigerate until lemon gelatin layer is set, at least 90 minutes.
3. Pour remaining 3/4 cup boiling water into the small bowl. Add orange gelatin mix; stir until dissolved. Pour remaining 1 cup vodka into a glass measuring cup; add enough ice to make 1 1/4 cup. Stir into orange gelatin until slightly thickened; remove any unmelted ice. Pour over lemon gelatin layer.
4. Refrigerate until orange gelatin layer is set, at least 90 minutes.
5. Pour 2 tablespoons warm water into a bowl. Add unflavored gelatin; stir until dissolved. Stir in condensed milk and rum. Pour over orange gelatin layer.
6. Refrigerate until top layer is set, at least 30 minutes.

MIDORI GLOW

Servings: 1 | Prep: 2m | Cooks: 0m | Total: 2m

INGREDIENTS

- 1/2 cup ice cubes
- 1 fluid ounce melon liqueur
- 2 fluid ounces vodka
- 1 cup lemon-lime flavored carbonated beverage

DIRECTIONS

1. Fill a short glass with ice. Pour in vodka and melon liqueur, and stir. Top off with lemon lime soda, and serve.

TEXAS HURRICANE

Servings: 1 | Prep: 10m | Cooks: 0m | Total: 10m

INGREDIENTS

- 1 cup crushed ice
- 1 fluid ounce pineapple juice
- 1 fluid ounce rum
- 1 fluid ounce grenadine syrup
- 1 fluid ounce coconut flavored rum
- 1 fluid ounce 151 proof rum
- 1 fluid ounce vodka
- 1 orange slice (optional)
- 1 fluid ounce gin
- 1 lime slice (optional)
- 1 fluid ounce triple sec (orange-flavored liqueur)
- 1 maraschino cherry (optional)
- 2 fluid ounces orange juice

DIRECTIONS

1. Fill a hurricane glass with ice. Pour in the rum, coconut rum, vodka, gin, triple sec, orange juice, pineapple juice, and grenadine. Stir well with a bar spoon, then pour the 151 rum over the back of the spoon to float the liquor on top of the drink. Garnish the glass with orange, lime, and a cherry.
2. Sip with a straw from the bottom for a 'sneak up on you' punch or sip from the top for a 'knock you down' twister.

REDEYE BLOODY MARY

Servings: 16 | Prep: 30m | Cooks: 8h | Total: 8h30m

INGREDIENTS

- 2 1/2 quarts tomato juice
- 1 1/4 teaspoons celery salt
- 3 cups vodka
- 2 teaspoons hot pepper sauce (such as Frank's RedHot)
- 1 cup fresh lemon juice
- 1 tablespoon ground black pepper
- 1/2 cup fresh lime juice
- 1/4 cup pickled pepper juice
- 1/4 cup prepared horseradish
- 1/2 cup chopped fresh cilantro
- 1/4 cup Worcestershire sauce

DIRECTIONS

1. Combine the tomato juice, vodka, lemon juice, lime juice, horseradish, Worcestershire sauce, celery salt, hot pepper sauce, black pepper, and pickled pepper juice in a large pitcher; stir. Refrigerate 8 hours to overnight. Stir in cilantro just before serving.

MELONADE

Servings: 1 | Prep: 5m | Cooks: 0m | Total: 5m

INGREDIENTS

- 1 cup ice cubes
- 1 fluid ounce vodka
- 2 (1.5 fluid ounce) jiggers melon liqueur
- 2 fluid ounces lemon-lime soda
- 2 fluid ounces sweet and sour mix

DIRECTIONS

1. Fill a tumbler with ice cubes and pour in the melon liqueur, sour mix, vodka, and lemon-lime soda. Stir to mix.

JEDI MIND TRICK

Servings: 1 | Prep: 5m | Cooks: 0m | Total: 5m

INGREDIENTS

- 1/2 fluid ounce spiced rum
- 3/4 fluid ounce amaretto liqueur
- 1/2 fluid ounce Irish cream liqueur
- 1/2 cup half-and-half or vanilla ice cream
- 3/4 fluid ounce coffee flavored liqueur

DIRECTIONS

1. Fill a large glass with ice. Pour in the spiced rum, Irish cream, coffee liqueur and amaretto. Fill the rest of the glass with half and half, or vanilla ice cream.

FRESH-SQUEEZED SALTY DOG
Servings: 1 | Prep: 10m | Cooks: 0m | Total: 10m

INGREDIENTS

- 1 grapefruit, juiced
- 1 (1.5 fluid ounce) jigger gin
- salt to taste

DIRECTIONS

1. Shake together the grapefruit juice, gin, and a generous amount of salt in a cocktail shaker. Pour into a glass over ice.

ITALIAN AMARETTO MARGARITAS ON THE ROCKS
Servings: 4 | Prep: 5m | Cooks: 0m | Total: 5m

INGREDIENTS

- 2 tablespoons confectioners' sugar
- 5 fluid ounces amaretto (almond-flavored liqueur)
- 4 cups crushed ice
- 2 fluid ounces orange liqueur
- 2 cups sweet and sour mix
- 4 orange slices for garnish
- 5 fluid ounces tequila
- 4 lime slices for garnish

DIRECTIONS

1. Slightly moisten rims of 4 12-ounce glasses and dip in confectioners' sugar to rim the glasses; fill each with crushed ice.
2. Combine the sweet and sour mix, tequila, amaretto, and orange liqueur in a pitcher; stir. Pour mixture into the prepared glasses. Garnish each drink with orange and lime slices.

DON'S FRIEND TONJA'S COUSIN TONI'S BOYFRIEND'S GRANDMOTHER'S EGGNOG

Servings: 16 | Prep: 15m | Cooks: 8h | Total: 15m

INGREDIENTS

- 6 eggs
- 2 quarts half-and-half cream
- 1 1/4 cups white sugar
- 2 teaspoons ground nutmeg, or amount to taste
- 1 quart bourbon
- 1 pint heavy whipping cream
- 1 cup rum

DIRECTIONS

1. In a large bowl, beat the eggs and sugar with an electric mixer until thick and pale, about 5 minutes. Gradually stir in the bourbon, rum, half and half and nutmeg.
2. In a separate chilled bowl, whip the cream until it can stand in a peak. Fold the whipped cream into the egg mixture. Pour into a plastic container and refrigerate overnight (if possible). Shake the container before serving.

FIZZY LIME VODKA PRESS

Servings: 1 | Prep: 5m | Cooks: 0m | Total: 5m

INGREDIENTS

- 1 1/2 fluid ounces lemon flavored vodka
- 2 slices lemon
- 4 fluid ounces club soda
- 2 slices lime
- 1/2 fluid ounce cola-flavored carbonated beverage

DIRECTIONS

1. Fill a highball glass with ice; add vodka, club soda, cola, lemon wedges, and lime wedges; stir.

HOT IRISH WHISKEY

Servings: 1 | Prep: 10m | Cooks: 0m | Total: 10m

INGREDIENTS

- 8 whole cloves
- 3/4 cup boiling water
- 1 (1/4 inch thick) slice of lemon
- 1 (1.5 fluid ounce) jigger Irish whiskey
- 1 tablespoon white sugar

DIRECTIONS

1. Press cloves into the peel of the lemon slice all the way around. Set aside. Measure the sugar into a wine glass. Place a metal spoon into the glass with the curved side facing upwards. Pour the boiling water over the back of the spoon. This will keep your wine glass from shattering. Stir to dissolve the sugar. Pour in the whiskey and add the lemon slice. Let steep for about 1 minute before drinking.

HOP, SKIP AND GO NAKED

Servings: 1 | Prep: 5m | Cooks: 0m | Total: 5m

INGREDIENTS

- 1 (1.5 fluid ounce) jigger cherry vodka
- 1 dash grenadine syrup
- 1 (1.5 fluid ounce) jigger triple sec
- 4 fluid ounces cranberry juice

DIRECTIONS

1. Pour the vodka, triple sec, grenadine, and cranberry juice into a cocktail shaker over ice. Cover, and shake until the outside of the shaker has frosted. Strain into a chilled martini glass to serve.

WHITE RUSSIAN ..BECAUSE JOE PERRY DRANK THEM

Servings: 6 | Prep: m | Cooks: m | Total: m

INGREDIENTS

- 1 cup ice cubes
- 1 fluid ounce vodka
- 1 fluid ounce coffee flavored liqueur
- 1 fluid ounce heavy cream

DIRECTIONS

1. Place the ice cubes in a highball glass, or one of similar size. Pour the coffee, vodka and cream over the ice. Stir and serve. No garnishes here.

BEE'S KNEES

Servings: 10 | Prep: 10m | Cooks: 0m | Total: 10m

INGREDIENTS

- 1 (46 fluid ounce) can pineapple juice
- 1 (8 ounce) jar honey
- 1 (46 fluid ounce) can grapefruit juice
- 2 cups gin

DIRECTIONS

1. In a blender combine pineapple juice, grapefruit juice, honey and gin. Blend until frothy. Pour into a pitcher and serve.

BUSHWACKER

Servings: 1 | Prep: 2m | Cooks: 0m | Total: 2m

INGREDIENTS

- 2 fluid ounces coffee flavored liqueur
- 2 fluid ounces amaretto liqueur
- 2 fluid ounces coconut rum
- 2 fluid ounces cream of coconut
- 2 fluid ounces Irish cream liqueur
- 1 pinch ground nutmeg
- 2 fluid ounces vodka

DIRECTIONS

1. In a one-quart blender half filled with ice, combine coffee liqueur, rum, Irish cream, vodka, amaretto and coconut cream. Blend until smooth. Pour into cup and sprinkle a little nutmeg on top and enjoy a little taste of the Islands.

MARTINI

Servings: 1 | Prep: 2m | Cooks: 0m | Total: 2m

INGREDIENTS

- 2 1/2 fluid ounces gin
- 1 pitted green olive
- 1/2 fluid ounce dry vermouth
- 1 cup ice

DIRECTIONS

1. Scoop ice into a shaker. Pour in gin and vermouth. Cover shaker, and gently shake to mix vermouth and gin. Pour drink, without ice, into a cocktail glass. Gently drop olive or lemon twist into the glass. Serve.

MY FATHER'S LIME DAIQUIRI

Servings: 4 | Prep: 10m | Cooks: 0m | Total: 10m

INGREDIENTS

- 3 limes, juiced
- 4 maraschino cherries
- 1/2 cup white sugar
- 6 cups ice cubes
- 10 fluid ounces white rum

DIRECTIONS

1. In a blender combine lime juice, sugar and rum. Blend and add ice one cube at a time until mixture is thick and smooth. Pour into 4 glasses and garnish with maraschino cherries.

SHAGGY'S HANA BAY FROOTIE JOY

Servings: 2 | Prep: 1m | Cooks: 0m | Total: 1m

INGREDIENTS

- 4 fluid ounces rum
- 4 cubes ice
- 1 cup fresh coconut-pineapple juice

DIRECTIONS

1. Fill 2 tall glasses half full with ice. Pour 2 ounces of rum in each. Fill the glasses with fresh coconut-pineapple juice. Stir and enjoy the sunset.

MOJITO COCKTAIL

Servings: 1 | Prep: 1m | Cooks: 0m | Total: 1m

INGREDIENTS

- 2 leaves fresh mint
- 1 1/4 fluid ounces rum
- 1 tablespoon simple syrup
- 1 fluid ounce carbonated water
- 2 cubes ice
- 1 sprig fresh mint

DIRECTIONS

1. In a cocktail glass, muddle (crush) mint leaves with simple syrup. Add ice and rum. Top with carbonated water. Garnish with a sprig of fresh mint.

PARADISE ISLAND

Servings: 2 | Prep: 2m | Cooks: 0m | Total: 2m

INGREDIENTS

- 1 cup coconut flavored rum
- 1/2 cup grapefruit juice
- 1/2 cup orange juice
- 2 tablespoons frozen strawberries

DIRECTIONS

1. In a blender, combine coconut rum, orange juice, grapefruit juice and frozen strawberries. Blend until smooth. Pour into glass and serve.
2. In a cocktail mixer, combine coconut rum, orange juice and grapefruit juice. Mix well and pour into glasses. Garnish with frozen strawberries.

CANDY CANE MARTINI

Servings: 1 | Prep: 5m | Cooks: 0m | Total: 5m

INGREDIENTS

- 3 fluid ounces rum
- 1/2 fluid ounce grenadine syrup
- 2 fluid ounces peppermint schnapps
- 1 small candy cane

DIRECTIONS

1. Pour the rum, schnapps, and grenadine into a cocktail shaker over ice. Cover, and shake until the outside of the shaker has frosted. Strain into a chilled martini glass, and garnish with the candy cane to serve.

RUDOLPH-TINI

Servings: 1 | Prep: 5m | Cooks: 0m | Total: 5m

INGREDIENTS

- 2 fluid ounces vodka
- 1 fluid ounce half-and-half cream
- 1 fluid ounce hazelnut liqueur, such as Frangelico
- 2 (4 inch) cinnamon sticks
- 1 fluid ounce coconut flavored rum
- 1 maraschino cherry

DIRECTIONS

1. Pour the vodka, hazelnut liqueur, rum, and half-and-half into a cocktail shaker over ice. Cover, and shake until the outside of the shaker has frosted. Strain into a chilled martini glass; garnish with the cinnamon sticks to look like antlers, and the cherry on the rim to look like a nose.

BILL'S FAMOUS PINA COLADA

Servings: 2 | Prep: 5m | Cooks: 0m | Total: 5m

NUTRITION FACTS

Calories: 641 | Carbohydrates: 81.8g | Fat: 16.6g | Protein: 1.2g | Cholesterol: 11mg

INGREDIENTS

- 1 fluid ounce light rum
- 2 fluid ounces cream of coconut (such as Coco Lopez)
- 1 fluid ounce amber rum
- 1 fluid ounce half-and-half cream
- 3 fluid ounces pineapple juice
- ice cubes, as needed
- 2 fluid ounces sweet and sour mix
- 1/4 fluid ounce dark rum (optional)

DIRECTIONS

1. Pour the light rum, amber rum, pineapple juice, sweet and sour mix, cream of coconut, and half-and-half cream into the pitcher of a blender with ice; blend until the cocktail has a slushy texture. Pour the slushy mixture into a glass.
2. Slowly and gently drizzle the dark rum over the drink so it just floats on top; serve.

CANDY APPLE MARTINI

Servings: 1 | Prep: 5m | Cooks: 0m | Total: 5m

INGREDIENTS

- 1 fluid ounce vanilla vodka
- 1 fluid ounce cranberry juice
- 1 fluid ounce sour apple schnapps
- 1 maraschino cherry
- 1 fluid ounce butterscotch schnapps

DIRECTIONS

1. Pour the vodka, apple schnapps, butterscotch schnapps, and cranberry juice into a cocktail shaker over ice. Cover, and shake until the outside of the shaker has frosted. Strain into a chilled martini glass, and garnish with a maraschino cherry to serve.

PUMPKIN PIE MARTINI

Servings: 1 | Prep: 5m | Cooks: 0m | Total: 5m

INGREDIENTS

- 1 graham cracker, crushed
- 3/4 (1.5 fluid ounce) jigger vanilla flavored vodka
- 1 tablespoon honey
- 1/2 (1.5 fluid ounce) jigger creme de cacao
- 1/3 cup milk
- 1 pinch pumpkin pie spice
- 2 tablespoons pumpkin puree
- 1 cup crushed ice

DIRECTIONS

1. Place graham cracker crumbs in a shallow dish. Coat rim of martini glass with honey, and dip into graham cracker crumbs to coat.
2. Combine milk and pumpkin puree in a cocktail shaker, and shake to combine. Pour in vodka and creme de cacao, and add ice. Shake well, and then strain into prepared martini glass. Garnish with a sprinkle of pumpkin pie spice.

FROZEN BANANA MARGARITAS

Servings: 8 | Prep: 15m | Cooks: 0m | Total: 15m

INGREDIENTS

- 2 tablespoons lemon juice
- 1/4 cup triple sec (orange-flavored liqueur)
- 2 tablespoons lime juice
- 6 ice cubes
- 3/4 cup banana liqueur
- 2 large bananas
- 1/2 cup tequila

DIRECTIONS

1. In the container of a blender, combine the lemon juice, lime juice, banana liqueur, tequila, triple sec, and bananas. Add ice cubes until the mixture reaches the 6 cup line. Cover and blend until smooth. Pour into margarita glasses to serve.

RUSSIAN QUAALUDE

Servings: 1 | Prep: 3m | Cooks: 0m | Total: 3m

INGREDIENTS

- Ice cubes
- 1 fluid ounce Irish cream liqueur
- 1 fluid ounce coffee liqueur
- 1 fluid ounce hazelnut liqueur, such as Frangelico
- 1 fluid ounce vodka
- 1 fluid ounce half-and-half

DIRECTIONS

1. Fill a highball glass with ice. Pour in coffee liqueur, vodka, Irish cream, hazelnut liqueur and half-and-half. Stir with a cocktail stirrer.

LYNCHBURG LEMONADE COCKTAIL

Servings: 1 | Prep: 5m | Cooks: 0m | Total: 5m

NUTRITION FACTS

Calories: 263 | Carbohydrates: 33.1g | Fat: 0.1g | Protein: 0.2g | Cholesterol: 0mg

INGREDIENTS

- 1 fluid ounce Tennessee whiskey (such as Jack Daniels)
- 1 1/2 cups ice
- 1 fluid ounce triple sec
- 2 fluid ounces lemon-lime soda
- 1 fluid ounce sweet and sour mix
- 1 lemon wheel

DIRECTIONS

1. Combine whiskey, triple sec, and sweet and sour mix in a pint glass. Add ice and top with lemon lime soda.
2. Garnish with lemon wheel.

PINA COLADA COCKTAIL

Servings: 1 | Prep: 5m | Cooks: 0m | Total: 5m

NUTRITION FACTS

Calories: 423 | Carbohydrates: 37.4g | Fat: 9.3g | Protein: 0.9g | Cholesterol: 0mg

INGREDIENTS

- 3 fluid ounces light rum
- 3 tablespoons crushed pineapple
- 3 tablespoons cream of coconut
- 2 cups ice

DIRECTIONS

1. Combine rum, cream of coconut, pineapple, and ice in a blender. Puree on high speed until smooth. Pour into chilled Collins glass and serve with a straw.

TEQUILA SUNRISE COCKTAIL

Servings: 1 | Prep: 5m | Cooks: 0m | Total: 5m

NUTRITION FACTS

Calories: 263 | Carbohydrates: 31.8g | Fat: 0.2g | Protein: 0.9g | Cholesterol: 0mg

INGREDIENTS

- 1 1/2 cups ice

- 1 cup ice
- 2 fluid ounces tequila
- 3/4 fluid ounce grenadine syrup
- 4 fluid ounces orange juice

DIRECTIONS

1. Fill a highball glass with 1 1/2 cups ice and set aside.
2. Combine tequila and orange juice in a cocktail mixing glass. Add 1 cup ice, stir, and strain into the prepared highball glass. Slowly pour in grenadine and let settle.
3. Stir before drinking.

PRICKLY PEAR CACTUS MARGARITA

Servings: 1 | Prep: 10m | Cooks: 0m | Total: 10m

NUTRITION FACTS

Calories: 423 | Carbohydrates: 56.3g | Fat: 0.1g | Protein: 0.1g | Cholesterol: 0mg

INGREDIENTS

- coarse salt as needed
- 1 fluid ounce triple sec
- 2 fluid ounces tequila
- 1 fluid ounce lime juice
- 2 fluid ounces sweet and sour mix
- 1 fluid ounce prickly pear syrup

DIRECTIONS

1. Pour salt into a small plate. Wet the rim of a margarita glass and dip rim into salt.
2. Fill a cocktail shaker with ice; pour tequila, sweet and sour mix, triple sec, lime juice, and pear syrup over ice. Cover shaker and shake drink; strain into prepared margarita glass.

MAGNIFICENT FROZEN MANGO MARGARITAS

Servings: 4 | Prep: 10m | Cooks: 0m | Total: 10m

NUTRITION FACTS

Calories: 220 | Carbohydrates: 34g | Fat: 0.2g | Protein: 0.3g | Cholesterol: 0mg

INGREDIENTS

- 1 cup ice, or as needed

- 3 fluid ounces ginger ale (such as Vernors)
- 1 cup frozen mango chunks
- 3 fluid ounces simple syrup
- 3 fluid ounces tequila
- 1 1/2 fluid ounces lemon juice
- 3 fluid ounces triple sec

DIRECTIONS

1. Blend ice, mango, tequila, triple sec, ginger ale, simple syrup, and lemon juice in a blender until smooth.

PRESIDENTE MARGARITA

Servings: 1 | Prep: 5m | Cooks: 0m | Total: 5m

NUTRITION FACTS

Calories: 416 | Carbohydrates: 55.4g | Fat: 0.1g | Protein: 0.1g | Cholesterol: 0mg

INGREDIENTS

- salt for rimming glass
- 1/2 fluid ounce orange-flavored liqueur (such as Cointreau)
- 3 cubes ice, or as desired
- 1/2 fluid ounce brandy (such as Presidente)
- 4 fluid ounces sweet-and-sour cocktail mix
- 1 splash lime juice
- 1 1/4 fluid ounces tequila

DIRECTIONS

1. Rim a margarita glass with salt; place ice into glass. Pour cocktail mix, tequila, orange liqueur, brandy, and lime juice into a cocktail shaker, cover, and shake to combine. Pour into prepared glass.

HOMEMADE OLD FASHIONED MIX

Servings: 48 | Prep: 10m | Cooks: 1h | Total: 1h10m

NUTRITION FACTS

Calories: 66 | Carbohydrates: 15.8g | Fat: 0g | Protein: 0g | Cholesterol: 0mg

INGREDIENTS

- 3 cups water

- 5 maraschino cherries, or more to taste
- 3 cups white sugar
- 1 cinnamon stick
- 3 clementine oranges, quartered
- 2 tablespoons bitters, or to taste

DIRECTIONS

1. Bring water and sugar to a boil in a saucepan; remove from heat. Stir oranges, cherries, and cinnamon stick into sugar mixture. Cover saucepan and steep for 1 hour.
2. Remove fruit and cinnamon stick from mixture using a slotted spoon; stir in bitters.

BLOODY MARY COCKTAIL

Servings: 1 | Prep: 5m | Cooks: 0m | Total: 5m

NUTRITION FACTS

Calories: 126 | Carbohydrates: 7.1g | Fat: 0.2g | Protein: 1.3g | Cholesterol: 0mg

INGREDIENTS

- 1 1/2 cups ice cubes
- 2 dashes Worcestershire sauce
- 4 fluid ounces tomato juice
- 1 pinch salt and ground black pepper
- 1 1/2 fluid ounces vodka
- ice
- 1/4 fluid ounce fresh lemon juice
- 1 stalk celery, for garnish
- 4 dashes hot pepper sauce (such as Tabasco)

DIRECTIONS

1. Fill a pint glass or goblet with 1 1/2 cups ice. Set aside.
2. Combine tomato juice, vodka, lemon juice, hot pepper sauce, Worcestershire sauce, salt, black pepper, and 1 cup ice in a mixing glass. Stir until chilled and strain into ice-filled pint glass or goblet.
3. Garnish with a celery stalk.

HOT TODDY COCKTAIL

Servings: 1 | Prep: 5m | Cooks: 0m | Total: 5m

NUTRITION FACTS

Calories: 204 | Carbohydrates: 17.7g | Fat: 0g | Protein: 0.1g | Cholesterol: 0mg

INGREDIENTS

- 3/4 cup hot water
- 3/4 cup hot water
- 1 tablespoon honey
- 1 twist lemon peel
- 2 fluid ounces bourbon whiskey

DIRECTIONS

1. Preheat an Irish coffee glass with 3/4 cup hot water, then discard.
2. Pour honey and bourbon into the preheated glass and top with 3/4 cup hot water. Garnish with a lemon twist.

ALCOHOLIC SWEET PEACH TEA

Servings: 1 | Prep: 5m | Cooks: 0m | Total: 5m

NUTRITION FACTS

Calories: 173 | Carbohydrates: 14g | Fat: 0.1g | Protein: 0g | Cholesterol: 0mg

INGREDIENTS

- ice cubes
- 1 fluid ounce vodka
- 1 cup iced tea
- 1 fluid ounce peach schnapps

DIRECTIONS

1. Fill a tall glass with ice. Pour iced tea, vodka, and peach schnapps over the ice.

CANDY CANE DRINKS

Servings: 16 | Prep: 10m | Cooks: 1h | Total: 1h10m

NUTRITION FACTS

Calories: 370 | Carbohydrates: 38.8g | Fat: 13.9g | Protein: 3.6g | Cholesterol: 44mg

INGREDIENTS

- 16 fluid ounces peppermint schnapps
- 1 splash grenadine syrup

- 16 fluid ounces white creme de cacao
- 16 small candy canes
- 2 quarts half-and-half

DIRECTIONS

1. Mix schnapps, creme de cacao, half-and-half, and grenadine together in a pitcher; refrigerate until chilled, at least 1 hour.
2. Stir mixture before pouring into martini glasses to serve; garnish each glass with a candy cane.

BAILEYS S'MORES

Servings: 1 | Prep: 10m | Cooks: 0m | Total: 10m

NUTRITION FACTS

Calories: 494 | Carbohydrates: 79.5g | Fat: 1.2g | Protein: 1.3g | Cholesterol: 0mg

INGREDIENTS

- 3 ounces Baileys Original Irish Cream
- Chocolate sauce
- Crushed graham crackers
- Large marshmallows
- Mini marshmallows

DIRECTIONS

1. Crush and then layer graham crackers at the bottom of a mason jar or cup.
2. Add a layer of mini marshmallows and chocolate sauce (proportion and layer to your taste). Top with a few large marshmallows.
3. Drizzle 3 oz. of Baileys Original Irish Cream on top for a sweet finish. Brown marshmallows with a creme brulee torch.

LEMON WHISKEY SLUSH

Servings: 4 | Prep: 5m | Cooks: 0m | Total: 5m

INGREDIENTS

- 1/2 cup Irish whiskey
- 1/2 cup fresh lemon juice
- 3 tablespoons white sugar
- 4 cups ice cubes

DIRECTIONS

1. In the container of a blender, combine the Irish whiskey, sugar, lemon juice and ice cubes. Cover and blend until slushy, 15 to 30 seconds. Pour into glasses and serve.

DAN FAY MARTINI

Servings: 2 | Prep: 5m | Cooks: 0m | Total: 5m

INGREDIENTS

- 2 fluid ounces vodka
- 2 twists lemon peel
- 1 1/2 fluid ounces gin
- 4 pimento-stuffed green olives
- ice cubes

DIRECTIONS

1. Measure the vodka and gin into a cocktail shaker and add a generous scoop of ice cubes. Secure the lid and shake until the outside of the shaker becomes frosty cold. Strain into two martini glasses. Garnish each drink with two olives speared on cocktail picks and a twist of lemon.

RICKYROOTBEER

Servings: 1 | Prep: 5m | Cooks: 0m | Total: 5m

INGREDIENTS

- 1/2 fluid ounce vanilla vodka
- 1/2 fluid ounce Irish cream liqueur
- 4 fluid ounces root beer

DIRECTIONS

1. Pour the vodka and Irish cream into a shot glass. Pour the root beer into a tumbler. Drop the entire shot glass into the root beer and drink immediately.

POPPED CHERRY

Servings: 1 | Prep: 5m | Cooks: 0m | Total: 5m

INGREDIENTS

- 1 cup ice
- 4 fluid ounces orange juice
- 1 fluid ounce maraschino cherry juice

- 3 maraschino cherries
- 2 fluid ounces vodka

DIRECTIONS

1. Fill a highball glass with ice, and pour in the cherry juice, vodka, and orange juice. Stir to mix, and garnish with maraschino cherries to serve.

PERFECT PITCHER OF PINK RASPBERRY COSMOPOLITANS

Servings: 10 | Prep: 10m | Cooks: 0m | Total: 10m

INGREDIENTS

- 1 cup raspberry vodka
- 3 cups cran-raspberry juice
- 1/2 cup triple sec
- 1 lime, sliced
- 1/2 cup sweetened lime juice (such as Rose's)

DIRECTIONS

1. Fill a pitcher with ice, and pour in the vodka, triple sec, lime juice, and cran-raspberry juice. Stir to mix. Serve garnished with a lime slice that has been rubbed around the glass edge.

DAVE MATTHEWS

Servings: 1 | Prep: 5m | Cooks: 0m | Total: 5m

INGREDIENTS

- 1 fluid ounce coconut-flavored rum
- 3/4 fluid ounce pineapple juice
- 1 fluid ounce amaretto liqueur
- 1/2 fluid ounce cranberry juice
- 1/4 fluid ounce fresh lime juice

DIRECTIONS

1. Pour the rum, amaretto, lime juice, pineapple juice, and cranberry juice into a tall glass with ice; stir.

IRISH SPRITZER

Servings: 1 | Prep: 5m | Cooks: 0m | Total: 5m

INGREDIENTS

- 2 fluid ounces club soda
- 1 fluid ounce amaretto liqueur
- ice
- 1 fluid ounce Irish cream liqueur

DIRECTIONS

1. Pour the club soda into a short glass over the ice cubes. Add the amaretto and Irish cream liqueurs and stir.

THE PERFECT BLENDED MARGARITA
Servings: 4 | Prep: 10m | Cooks: 0m | Total: 10m

INGREDIENTS

- 1 1/4 cups fresh lime juice
- 3 tablespoons fresh lemon juice
- 1 cup Triple Sec or other orange liqueur
- 3 cups ice cubes
- 1 cup silver tequila

DIRECTIONS

1. Combine the lime juice, triple sec, tequila, lemon juice, and 2 cups ice in a blender; blend until smooth.
2. Place 1 cup ice cubes in a cocktail shaker; add desired amount of margarita; cover and shake well; serve.

SCREWRITA
Servings: 1 | Prep: 5m | Cooks: 0m | Total: 5m

INGREDIENTS

- 1/2 cup ice
- 1/2 fluid ounce triple sec
- 1/2 cup orange juice
- 1 teaspoon sugar
- 1 fluid ounce tequila
- 1 dash fresh lime juice

DIRECTIONS

1. Fill a glass with ice. Pour the orange juice, tequila, triple sec, sugar, and lime juice over the ice; stir.

LAVA FLOW

Servings: 1 | Prep: 5m | Cooks: 0m | Total: 5m

INGREDIENTS

- 1/2 cup strawberries
- 1 banana
- 1 fluid ounce light rum
- 2 fluid ounces pineapple juice
- 1 fluid ounce coconut rum
- 2 fluid ounces cream of coconut

DIRECTIONS

1. Place strawberries, light rum, and dark rum into a blender. Puree until smooth and pour into a tall glass. Rinse out blender, then puree banana, pineapple juice, and cream of coconut until smooth. Slowly pour the banana mixture into the strawberry mixture and watch the lava rise

ROOT BEER PARALYZER

Servings: 1 | Prep: 1m | Cooks: 0m | Total: 1m

INGREDIENTS

- 1 fluid ounce coffee flavored liqueur
- 3 1/2 fluid ounces cola-flavored carbonated beverage
- 1/2 fluid ounce root beer schnapps
- ice
- 4 fluid ounces milk

DIRECTIONS

1. Fill a tall glass with ice. Pour in coffee liqueur, root beer schnapps and milk. Top with cola.

B-52 BOMBER

Servings: 1 | Prep: 1m | Cooks: 0m | Total: 1m

INGREDIENTS

- 1 tablespoon Kahlua or other coffee flavored liqueur
- 1 tablespoon brandy-based orange liqueur (such as Grand Marnier)

- 1 tablespoon Irish cream liqueur

DIRECTIONS

1. Carefully pour coffee liqueur, Grand Marnier, and Irish cream liqueur into a cordial glass so that they do not mix.

WORLD'S GREATEST MARTINI

Servings: 4 | Prep: 3m | Cooks: 0m | Total: 3m

INGREDIENTS

- 8 fluid ounces gin
- 4 cups ice cubes
- 1/2 fluid ounce dry vermouth
- 4 pimento-stuffed green olives
- 1/2 fluid ounce sweet vermouth

DIRECTIONS

1. Fill cocktail shaker with fresh ice cubes. Add about 1/2 ounce each dry and sweet vermouth. Shake enough to coat ice and pour off liquid. Add eight ounces gin to coated ice in shaker and shake vigorously. Pour into four chilled Martini glasses, garnish with pimiento-stuffed olive and serve.

ALABAMA SLAMMER

Servings: 1 | Prep: 2m | Cooks: 0m | Total: 2m

INGREDIENTS

- 1 fluid ounce Southern Comfort liqueur
- 1 dash grenadine syrup
- 1 fluid ounce amaretto liqueur
- 4 fluid ounces orange juice

DIRECTIONS

1. In a glass of ice, combine Southern Comfort, amaretto and grenadine. Fill with orange juice and stir.

STOLI O COSMO

Servings: 1 | Prep: 2m | Cooks: 0m | Total: 2m

INGREDIENTS

- 3 fluid ounces vodka
- 1 teaspoon fresh lime juice
- 1 tablespoon triple sec liqueur
- 1 tablespoon cranberry juice

DIRECTIONS

1. In a cocktail mixer full of ice, combine vodka, triple sec, lime juice and cranberry juice. Shake vigorously and strain into a cocktail glass. Garnish with a twist of lime.

CAPE BREEZE

Servings: 1 | Prep: 3m | Cooks: 0m | Total: 3m

INGREDIENTS

- 1 (1.5 fluid ounce) jigger coconut flavored rum
- 2 fluid ounces grapefruit juice
- 2 fluid ounces cranberry juice
- 1/2 teaspoon superfine sugar

DIRECTIONS

1. In a highball glass over ice, combine coconut rum, cranberry juice, grapefruit juice and sugar. Stir.

GRATEFUL DEAD

Servings: 1 | Prep: 5m | Cooks: 0m | Total: 5m

INGREDIENTS

- 1/4 fluid ounce vodka
- 1/4 fluid ounce triple sec liqueur
- 1/4 fluid ounce rum
- 1/4 fluid ounce raspberry flavored liqueur
- 1/4 fluid ounce tequila
- 2 fluid ounces cola-flavored carbonated beverage

DIRECTIONS

1. In a rocks glass over ice, combine vodka, rum, tequila, triple sec and raspberry liqueur. top with cola to taste.

MARGARITAS WITH A BITE

Servings: 4 | Prep: 7m | Cooks: 0m | Total: 7m

INGREDIENTS

- 8 (1.5 fluid ounce) jiggers gold tequila
- 3/4 (12 fluid ounce) can frozen limeade concentrate
- 4 (1.5 fluid ounce) jiggers triple sec
- 4 cups ice

DIRECTIONS

1. In a blender, combine tequila, triple sec and limeade concentrate. Fill blender to the top with ice. Blend, adding additional ice while blending, until thick and smooth. Pour into glasses and serve.

PINA COLADA

Servings: 4 | Prep: 10m | Cooks: 0m | Total: 10m

INGREDIENTS

- 3/4 cup sweetened cream of coconut
- 1 cup white rum
- 1/4 cup half-and-half cream
- 4 cups ice
- 1/2 cup pineapple juice
- 4 maraschino cherries

DIRECTIONS

1. In a blender, combine coconut cream, half-and-half, pineapple juice and rum. While blending, add ice a little at a time, until mixture is thick. Pour into 4 highball glasses, and garnish with cherries.

RO'S RUM RUNNER

Servings: 1 | Prep: 2m | Cooks: 0m | Total: 2m

INGREDIENTS

- 1 1/4 fluid ounces rum
- 1 1/2 fluid ounces orange juice
- 1/4 fluid ounce coconut flavored rum
- 1 dash grenadine syrup
- 1/2 fluid ounce banana liqueur
- 1 wedge orange, garnish

- 1/2 fluid ounce blackberry brandy
- 1 wedge lime, garnish
- 2 fluid ounces sweet and sour mix

DIRECTIONS

1. In a tall glass full of ice, pour rum, coconut rum, banana liqueur and blackberry brandy. Fill glass with sour mix and orange juice, then top with a dash of grenadine. Garnish with wedges of orange and lime.

LEMON KAMIKAZE

Servings: 1 | Prep: 5m | Cooks: 0m | Total: 5m

NUTRITION FACTS

Calories: 427 | Carbohydrates: 43g | Fat: 0.3g | Protein: 0.3g | Cholesterol: 0mg

INGREDIENTS

- 1 (1.5 fluid ounce) jigger vanilla vodka
- 1 fluid ounce lemon juice
- 1 (1.5 fluid ounce) jigger triple sec
- 1/2 fluid ounce lime juice
- 1 (1.5 fluid ounce) jigger limoncello liqueur
- 1 lemon twist

DIRECTIONS

1. Pour the vodka, triple sec, limoncello, lemon juice, and lime juice into a cocktail shaker over ice. Cover, and shake until the outside of the shaker has frosted. Strain into a chilled martini glass, and garnish with a twist of lemon to serve.

BEEFY BLOODY CAESAR

Servings: 1 | Prep: 5m | Cooks: 0m | Total: 5m

INGREDIENTS

- 1 pinch celery salt
- 1 dash dry beef bouillon powder
- ice cubes
- 1 dash hot pepper sauce
- 1 fluid ounce vodka
- 1 dash Worcestershire sauce

- 6 fluid ounces tomato and clam juice cocktail
- 1 stalk celery

DIRECTIONS

1. Rub the rim of a cocktail glass with celery salt. Place ice in the glass, and pour in vodka and tomato and clam juice cocktail. Mix in the bouillon powder, hot pepper sauce, and Worcestershire sauce. Garnish with celery.

CHOCOLATE BANANA MARTINI

Servings: 1 | Prep: 5m | Cooks: 0m | Total: 5m

INGREDIENTS

- 1 teaspoon chocolate syrup
- 1/3 cup milk
- 1 (1.5 fluid ounce) jigger banana liqueur
- 1 cup crushed ice
- 1 (1.5 fluid ounce) jigger coffee flavored liqueur
- 1/2 banana, peeled and sliced lengthwise into quarters

DIRECTIONS

1. Drizzle chocolate syrup round the inside of a martini glass.
2. Combine banana liqueur, coffee liqueur, milk, and ice in a shaker. Shake vigorously, and strain into martini glass. Garnish with banana spears.

STRAWBERRY CHEESECAKE MARTINI

Servings: 1 | Prep: 5m | Cooks: 0m | Total: 5m

INGREDIENTS

- 1 fluid ounce cranberry juice
- 1/2 fluid ounce grenadine syrup
- 1 fluid ounce vanilla flavored vodka
- 1 strawberry

DIRECTIONS

1. Pour the cranberry juice, vodka, and grenadine into a cocktail shaker over ice. Cover, and shake until the outside of the shaker has frosted. Strain into a chilled martini glass, and garnish with a strawberry on the rim of the glass to serve.

PISCO SOUR

Servings: 8 | Prep: 5m | Cooks: 0m | Total: 5m

INGREDIENTS

- 2 cups pisco
- 1 1/3 cups confectioners' sugar
- 1 cup fresh lime juice
- 2 cups crushed ice
- 1 egg white
- aromatic bitters

DIRECTIONS

1. Blend the pisco, lime juice, egg white, sugar, and ice in a blender until smooth, about 1 minute. Pour into fluted glasses and top each with 1 to 2 dashes of the aromatic bitters to serve.

PERFECT PEAR BRANDY SIDECAR

Servings: 1 | Prep: 5m | Cooks: 0m | Total: 5m

INGREDIENTS

- 1 (1.5 fluid ounce) jigger pear brandy
- 1/2 fluid ounce simple syrup
- 1/2 fluid ounce lemon juice
- 1 fluid ounce pear nectar

DIRECTIONS

1. Pour the brandy, lemon juice, simple syrup, and pear nectar into a cocktail shaker over ice. Cover, and shake until the outside of the shaker has frosted. Strain into a chilled martini glass to serve.

BOAT DRINK

Servings: 1 | Prep: 10m | Cooks: 0m | Total: 10m

NUTRITION FACTS

Calories: 341 | Carbohydrates: 46.1g | Fat: 0.3g | Protein: 0.5g | Cholesterol: 0mg

INGREDIENTS

- 1 (1.5 fluid ounce) jigger good quality silver tequila
- 1 splash lime juice

- 1/2 (1.5 fluid ounce) jigger melon liqueur (such as Midori)
- 1 (1.5 fluid ounce) jigger orange juice, or to taste
- 1/4 (1.5 fluid ounce) jigger triple sec
- 1 maraschino cherry for garnish
- 1/2 (1.5 fluid ounce) jigger sour mix
- 1 wedge orange for garnish
- 1 splash grenadine syrup

DIRECTIONS

1. Fill a margarita glass with crushed ice. Pour tequila, melon liqueur, and triple sec into the glass. Top with sour mix, grenadine, lime juice, and orange juice. Garnish with the cherry and a wedge of orange.

STRAWBERRYLICIOUS DAIQUIRIS

Servings: 4 | Prep: 5m | Cooks: 0m | Total: 5m

NUTRITION FACTS

Calories: 211 | Carbohydrates: 28g | Fat: 0g | Protein: 0.1g | Cholesterol: 0mg

INGREDIENTS

- 1 (1 pound) strawberries, halved
- 1/3 cup unsweetened pineapple juice
- 1/2 cup white sugar
- 3/4 cup spiced rum
- 1 tablespoon lime juice
- ice

DIRECTIONS

1. Combine strawberries and sugar in blender; blend until smooth. Pour in pineapple juice, lime juice, and rum. Pulse until combined. Serve over ice.

JOE'S PERFECT 'ANTI-SOUR MIX' MARGARITA

Servings: 1 | Prep: 10m | Cooks: 0m | Total: 10m

NUTRITION FACTS

Calories: 314 | Carbohydrates: 30.3g | Fat: 0.1g | Protein: 0g | Cholesterol: 0mg

INGREDIENTS

- kosher salt
- 1 fluid ounce orange liqueur
- 1 cup ice cubes
- 1 fluid ounce sweetened lime juice (such as Rose's)
- 2 fluid ounces silver tequila
- 2 ounces grapefruit flavored soda

DIRECTIONS

1. Pour 1/4 to 1/2 inch of salt onto a small, shallow plate. Moisten the rim of a large glass with water and dip into the salt. Fill the glass with ice, and set aside.
2. Pour the tequila, orange liqueur, and lime juice into a cocktail shaker over ice. Cover, and shake until the outside of the shaker has frosted. Strain into the prepared glass. Slowly pour in grapefruit soda to serve.

BANANA MONKEY

Servings: 1 | Prep: 5m | Cooks: 0m | Total: 5m

NUTRITION FACTS

Calories: 460 | Carbohydrates: 74.6g | Fat: 4.8g | Protein: 1.5g | Cholesterol: 0mg

INGREDIENTS

- 1 cup pina colada mix
- 1/3 banana, mashed
- 1 fluid ounce coffee-flavored liqueur (such as Kahlua)
- 1 cup ice cubes
- 1 fluid ounce vodka

DIRECTIONS

1. Place pina colada mix, coffee-flavored liqueur, vodka, banana, and 1/2 cup of ice into a blender. Cover, and puree until smooth. Add ice a little at a time and repeat until drink reaches desired consistency.

GOOD MOJITO

Servings: 1 | Prep: 5m | Cooks: 0m | Total: 5m

NUTRITION FACTS

Calories: 188 | Carbohydrates: 16.6g | Fat: 0.1g | Protein: 0.3g | Cholesterol: 0mg

INGREDIENTS

- 1/2 lime, juiced
- 2 fluid ounces white rum
- 1 tablespoon white sugar
- 4 fluid ounces soda water
- 5 mint leaves
- 1 lime wedge
- ice cubes

DIRECTIONS

1. Muddle the lime juice, sugar, and mint leaves together in the bottom of a cocktail glass until the mint has broken down a bit, about 1 minute. Fill the glass with ice cubes. Add the rum and soda water over the ice. Pour the mixture back and forth from from the glass to another glass to mix. Garnish with the lime wedge and enjoy.

LIQUID VALIUM

Servings: 4 | Prep: 5m | Cooks: 0m | Total: 5m

INGREDIENTS

- 2 cups ice cubes
- 3 fluid ounces coconut rum
- 1 cup whiskey (preferably Crown Royal)
- 2 fluid ounces orange juice
- 3 fluid ounces peach schnapps
- 2 fluid ounces cranberry juice

DIRECTIONS

1. Fill four glasses halfway full with ice. In a cocktail mixer full of ice, combine whiskey, peach schnapps, coconut rum, orange juice and cranberry juice. Shake vigorously and strain into glasses.

SOUTHERN COMFORT MANHATTAN

Servings: 1 | Prep: 5m | Cooks: 0m | Total: 5m

INGREDIENTS

- 2 (1.5 fluid ounce) jiggers Southern Comfort liqueur
- 4 ice cubes (optional)
- 1 (1.5 fluid ounce) jigger sweet vermouth
- 1 maraschino cherry
- 2 dashes aromatic bitters

DIRECTIONS

1. Fill a cocktail shaker with ice. Pour in the Southern Comfort, vermouth and aromatic bitters. Shake for about 15 seconds then strain into a highball glass with or without ice. Garnish with a maraschino cherry.

G-STREET SURPRISE

Servings: 2 | Prep: 5m | Cooks: 0m | Total: 5m

INGREDIENTS

- 1 cup frozen raspberries
- 3 (1.5 fluid ounce) jiggers citron vodka
- 1/2 cup frozen strawberries
- 1 cup lemonade

DIRECTIONS

1. Place raspberries, strawberries, vodka, and lemonade into a blender. Cover, and puree until smooth. Pour into chilled glasses to serve.

CALIMOCHO (KALIMOTXO)

Servings: 16 | Prep: 5m | Cooks: 0m | Total: 5m

INGREDIENTS

- 1 1/4 liters cola-flavored carbonated beverage
- 1 (750 milliliter) bottle red wine

DIRECTIONS

1. In a 1 gallon serving jar with a lid or in the 2 liter bottle from the cola, combine the cola and red wine. Put the lid on and gently rock the container to mix. Let rest for a few minutes before serving in glasses over ice.

BOBBING FOR APPLES

Servings: 1 | Prep: 2m | Cooks: 0m | Total: 2m

INGREDIENTS

- 1 cup ice cubes
- 2 fluid ounces Southern Comfort liqueur
- 1/4 cup apple cider, or as needed

DIRECTIONS

1. Fill a highball glass with ice. Pour in Southern Comfort, then fill the rest of the glass with apple cider. Stir before serving.

www.ingramcontent.com/pod-product-compliance
Lightning Source LLC
Chambersburg PA
CBHW081151130726
47996CB00009B/3078